The Food Lover's Trail Guide to Alberta

Volume Two

The

Food Lover's

TRAIL GUIDE TO ALBERTA

Volume Two

MARY BAILEY & JUDY SCHULTZ

BlueCOUCH**Books**

National Library of Canada Cataloguing in Publication
Bailey, Mary, (date)
The food lover's trail guide to Alberta : volume 2 / Mary Bailey &
Judy Schultz.

Includes index.
ISBN 1-894739-05-1

1. Food industry and trade--Alberta--Guidebooks. 2.
Restaurant--Alberta--
Guidebooks. 3. Alberta--Guidebooks. I. Schultz, Judy II. Title.

TX360.C32A52 2005   381'.456413'00257123   C2005-902171-3

Cover photos: J. Alleyne Photography
Map: Johnson Cartographics
All interior photos are by Mary Bailey except where indicated.

Blue Couch Books
an imprint of Brindle & Glass Publishing
www.bluecouchbooks.com

1 2 3 4 5 08 07 06 05

PRINTED AND BOUND IN CANADA

To the farmers and ranchers of Alberta, where good food starts.

*It's been a tough year for Alberta's farmers. Beef was hit with BSE,
borders were closed, elk and deer were threatened with CWD, bison
forbidden to cross the border, pork prices up and down like a yo-yo,
avian flu threatening poultry producers, a plague of grasshoppers,
and the weather doing its usual drought-to-flood routine.
It seemed that the sky was falling.*

*Yet the industry survives. As rancher and former agriculture minister Shirley McLellan
said during one of her many interviews, "We're still here, and we're still strong."*

Give thanks.

CONTENTS

SECTION ONE: The Food Lover's Trails

SECTION TWO: Artisans and Tastemakers

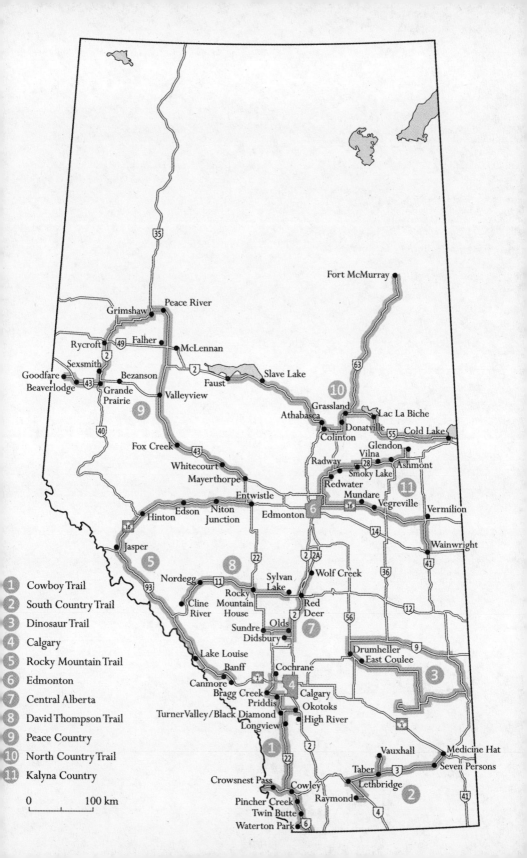

1 Cowboy Trail
2 South Country Trail
3 Dinosaur Trail
4 Calgary
5 Rocky Mountain Trail
6 Edmonton
7 Central Alberta
8 David Thompson Trail
9 Peace Country
10 North Country Trail
11 Kalyna Country

0   100 km

Fort McMurray

Grimshaw   Peace River
Rycroft   Falher   McLennan
Sexsmith
Goodfare   Bezanson
Beaverlodge   Grande   Valleyview
Prairie
Slave Lake
Faust

Fox Creek
Whitecourt
Mayerthorpe
Entwistle
Hinton   Edson   Niton   Edmonton
Junction
Jasper

Nordegg
Cline   Rocky
River   Mountain   Sylvan   Wolf Creek
House   Lake
Red
Sundre   Olds   Deer
Didsbury

Grassland
Athabasca   Lac La Biche
Donatville   Cold Lake
Colinton
Glendon
Vilna
Radway   Ashmont
Smoky Lake
Redwater
Mundare   Vegreville
Vermilion
Wainwright

Lake Louise
Banff
Canmore
Bragg Creek   Calgary
Priddis   Okotoks
Turner Valley/Black Diamond   High River
Longview

Drumheller
East Coulee

Vauxhall   Medicine Hat
Taber   Seven Persons
Crowsnest Pass   Cowley   Lethbridge
Pincher Creek   Raymond
Twin Butte
Waterton Park

Welcome to *The Food Lover's Trail Guide to Alberta, Volume Two.*

We're covering new ground. More of the Peace Country and the south, more of the mountains and central Alberta, more of the east. In this volume, we check out what's new on the city food scene. We find the best road food, great bars, food-lovin' festivals, and lots of reasons to take a Sunday drive.

As we travelled around the province last year, people would ask, with considerable amazement; "You ate in all these places?"

We were surprised that they were surprised.

This is a book about our personal experiences with food and the people who make it. Our search is for the authentic. It doesn't have to be haute cuisine. We like it simple and well-executed—flaky pie crust, great bread, the elusive perfectly poached egg.

We hunger for food that reflects our seasons—asparagus in May, fresh berries in August, root vegetable stew in January. We hunger for food that reflects our geography—wetlands, prairie, mountains and high country. We love our ethnic culinary landscape—the ubiquitous Greek steak and pizza and the Chinese café that's on every main street in Alberta. We love farms and farmers. A smiling dog with wagging tail is a welcome sight when we pull into the farmyard.

We also ate a lot of food that didn't make it into this book. For every spot that gets in, there are many that don't. We grill servers and chefs on where their beef comes from. If the burger patties are made at the butcher shop in the next town, we go to that butcher shop.

We've developed a shorthand in our travels: "No love here" means, well, there's no love here. No love for food, no respect for customers. A tragedy, in our opinion. "I could eat" means "interesting, let's check it out" (we say that a lot). We go off the road (quite literally) for signs that say "Homemade Pie One Mile." We get odd looks as we case the grocery aisles, exclaiming over the local beef or chicken, then leaving with nothing but a bottle of water. Pity the poor server who brings seven items to the table, only to watch us take one bite of each, ask for the cheque, steal the menu (if it's paper) and clear out.

Nobody knows we're coming. We pay for everything we eat.

In Volume Two, we tell more stories of intrepid ranchers and farmers who are changing the very nature of farming. We urge you to visit the farms in our books, hear their stories, taste their products, make a connection. We urge you to follow our trail. When you find places that make you say "I could eat," let us know. You can reach us at www.foodloversguide.ca.

Happy trails!

Judy and Mary

Food Lover's guides

Restaurant Listings

Every effort has been made to ensure that the information featured is accurate. However, prices, credit cards accepted and days and hours of operation could change. We have assumed all businesses take cash, and for those that don't take any other form of payment we've listed them as "cash only." Please call ahead to verify when making plans to visit a restaurant, store or event.

Pricing Symbols

$ under $10 for one person, without alcohol, tip or taxes

$$ under $20 for one person, without alcohol, tip or taxes

$$$ over $20 for one person, without alcohol, tip or taxes

The "R" symbol after the telephone number indicates that reservations are recommended.

Stores

Standard retail hours for most stores are 10:00 AM–6:00 PM, Monday through Saturday. Hours of operation are listed where available and applicable but are always subject to change. Please call ahead for verification.

Other Businesses

The producers, farmers and ranchers featured in this book operate enterprises that are affected by such things as the weather and the natural whims of livestock. Check out their web sites and call before visiting.

We've included phone numbers and web sites for producers who are set up for retail. To purchase products from the producers not set up for visitors, please inquire at your local grocery or health food stores, which often stock such items.

◎ If you have any comments or would like to tell us about a favourite producer, farmer, rancher, chef, restaurant or supplier not included here please send them by fax to (780) 433-0492 or by email to marybee@shaw.ca.

◎ This book is cross-referenced with the first *Food Lover's Trail Guide to Alberta*. Numbers following "V1" in the text and index refer to page numbers in Volume 1. Numbers in the "From Volume One We Still Like" sections also refer to page numbers in Volume 1. All other page numbers refer to this book.

For many people, the high country bordering the eastern slope of the Rockies defines Alberta. Historic, a little wild, with a rugged beauty all its own, this is an inspiring landscape.

We begin the Cowboy Trail north of Calgary on 144 Avenue, a road that scoots across the top of the city and an easy route through the hills to Cochrane.

⊚ CALGARY

$$ **Symon's Valley BBQ Ranch**
260011 Symons Valley Road NW   (403) 274-4574 R
Open Monday 4:00 PM–10:00 PM
Tuesday–Thursday 11:00 AM–10:00 PM
Friday, Saturday 11:00 AM–12:00 AM
V, MC, AE, DEBIT

It's Alberta beef in its natural rustic setting, nestled in the hills northwest of Calgary. More gathering place than actual restaurant, they love big crowds, cook with charcoal, and there's a limited menu of chicken, steak, roast beef, roast pork loin and southern-style barbecue ribs. With steak they serve beans, green salad and garlic bread, all on Chinet plates with plastic cutlery. Live bands Friday and Saturday. Catering is done outside or in the three big old log halls.

⊚ COCHRANE

Cochrane wears its cowboy heritage well. While driving Main Street on a Friday afternoon we were struck by the number of men decked out in full cowpoke regalia—pristine Stetsons, shiny boots, buckles as big as your head, even chaps. (The cowboys we know wear dusty jeans, old boots and a trucker cap.) We were curious about this glorious display of western sartorial splendor. "Where's the rodeo?" we asked our server, as we shook off the road dust with a Big Rock on the patio at the 100-year-old Rockyview Hotel.

We never did find an event. Maybe it was wear-your-chaps-to-work day. Or free beer for best belt buckle? We'll never know.

$$ **Canyon Rose Steakhouse, Rockyview Hotel**
Main Street   (403) 932-2442
Open daily 10:00 AM–2:00 PM, 5:00 PM–10:00 PM
V, MC, DEBIT

> This place is all about steak. Locally raised AAA beef; New York cuts range from an 8oz. Cowboy, through the Rancher's, the Trail Boss and the Cattlemen's, all the way to the Grande cut—20 oz. of serious beef. Other steaks in various sizes, plus an excellent buffalo ribeye, are available. Prime rib is the feature Friday and Saturday nights. Don't feel like beef? Try the mussels, veal, salmon, or even the cranberry walnut chicken.

$$ **Portofino Italian Ristorante**
Bay 18, 205 1st Street E (Cochrane Station)   (403) 932-1777 R
Open Tuesday–Friday 11:00 AM–2:00 PM, 5:00 PM–10:00 PM
Saturday, Sunday 4:00 PM–10:00 PM
V, MC, DEBIT

> Portofino's straightforward Italian repertoire of old favourites, fettucini alfredo, spaghetti bolognese, beef with peppercorn sauce and grilled Italian sausage are prepared with skill and heart. It's good classic Italian food. It's also the date place in town, according to the accommodating staff. During the summer the intimate patio is festooned with flowering baskets—altogether a lovely spot for a glass of wine and plate of pasta.

$ **Pho Anh Huyen II Vietnamese Noodle House**
8–312 5th Avenue W   (403) 932-8872
Open Sunday–Thursday 10:00 AM–8:00 PM
Friday, Saturday 10:00 AM–9:00 PM
V, MC, DEBIT

> We found this bustling noodle house, jam-packed with happy faces, in a large shopping mall in the new part of Cochrane. We ordered number 30C, the beef curry and chicken soup with vermicelli, and number 58, the stir-fried tofu with lemongrass, both tasty. The bestseller is the deep-fried spring rolls—we saw an order on every table.

The large menu covers off vermicelli, rice dishes, noodle soups, seafood with egg noodles and a selection of vegetarian dishes. Beverages include mango, durian, avocado, strawberry, jackfruit or lychee milkshakes and, of course, Vietnamese iced coffee. It's a great spot.

$ Donair on the Run

407A 1st Street W   (403) 932-2112
Open Monday–Thursday 11:00 AM–8:00 PM
Friday, Saturday 11:00 AM–10:00 PM; Sunday 12:00 PM–5:00 PM
DEBIT

The meat in this tiny, spotless shop is produced in Brooks to the owner's special recipe. It's leaner than most, yet still flavourful and juicy. The sauces—cucumber and yogurt-based tzatziki redolent of garlic and fresh herbs, a tahini (sesame) sauce, and the sweet donair sauce (the secret ingredient is evaporated milk)—are all delicious. You can have Syrian-style Middle Eastern specialties such as tabbouleh, hummus, pita and Mom's pastries. It's a family business: Dad owns the building, Mom makes the sauces, and Camille Elain, the son, owns and operates the shop. This is fast food worth stopping for.

$$ Blue Dog Café

110 3rd Avenue W   (403) 932-4282
Open daily 11:00 AM–11:00 PM
V, MC, DEBIT

We spent three trips looking in the wrong town for this excellent café. "Guess what, it's NOT in Canmore," said Marco to Polo. We stumbled in triumphant, sat at the bar, shared a smoky jambalaya with Spolumbo sausage and the crab

cakes that have become our personal favourites. It's a broad menu with a bit of everything, including Sunday breakfast.

The small, attractive room seats 34, with another 40 on the patio during the warmer months. Live music, friendly people, consistent quality. Expect lineups.

$$ **Coto Japanese Restaurant**

13–205 1st Street E (403) 932-2926 R

Open Sunday–Thursday 5:30 PM–9:00 PM

Friday, Saturday 5:30 PM–9:30 PM

V, MC, DEBIT

> Taeko and Shige Kamimori opened this jewel box of a restaurant just over two years ago. There are nine tables, no sushi bar. Starters include the lightly steamed edamame (soybeans in the pod) with sea salt and excellent calamari. We like the futo maki with vegetables, egg and dried fish and the ethereal tempura with seasonal vegetables. The Cochrane roll is made with ham and mayonnaise. For mains try the popular dong (bowls)—teriyaki chicken, salmon or beef.

PANTRY

Bernie's Bavarian Bakery

8–205 1st Street E (403) 932-9066

Open Tuesday–Friday 8:30 AM–5:30 PM

Saturday 9:00 AM–3:00 PM

> This is real artisan bread, using organic flours grown by the famous Nunweilers in Alsask, Saskatchewan. Bernie uses all-natural sourdoughs in his rye breads, and everything is baked in a stone-hearth oven. He also makes good cookies and a few pastries, but the bread's the thing.

Cochrane Coffee Traders

114 2nd Avenue (403) 932-1695

Open Monday–Wednesday, Friday 6:00 AM–6:00 PM

Thursday 6:00 AM–10:00 PM; Saturday 7:00 AM–6:00 PM; Sunday 9:00 AM–6:00 PM

117 River Avenue Roasterie (403) 932-4395

Monday–Friday 7:00 AM–1:30 PM

CASH

> The picturesque location just off Main Street is the place to enjoy a good cup of coffee and in-house baked goods. Jeff and Danielle Genung have built a sizeable business in wholesale coffee. Over at the roasterie and packing plant on River Avenue, there's coffee to go and a great selection of bagged whole-bean coffee.

$ **Boardwalk Café and Wine Bar**
Bragg Creek Shopping Centre (403) 949-2842
Open Monday–Friday 7:00 AM–7:00 PM; Saturday, Sunday 8:00 AM–7:00 PM
V, MC, AE, DEBIT

> They make an ethereal strudel, airy cakes and tortes—everything but the squares. Have coffee and sweets, or sign up for occasional wine dinners.

$$ **Infusion Contemporary Cuisine**
23 Balsam Avenue (403) 949-3898 R
Open daily 11:00 AM–10:00 PM (Seasonal changes, call first)
V, MC AE, DEBIT

> In a woodsy garden setting where chef Air Bouphasiry can grow his own herbs, you'll find some of the best food in Bragg Creek. He attempts an ambitious fusion of several cuisines—Asian and Mediterranean, French and North/South American. There's a roasted butternut squash soup flavoured with roasted red pepper coulis and Thai curry spices, and a creamy bisque of shitake mushrooms. We like the Malaysian grilled chicken and beef saté, the calamari, Thai-style—breaded, fried and served with a sweet spicy sauce. He serves New Zealand lamb (rack, with Dijon crust, rosemary merlot and fresh mint jus) and his beef is all AAA Alberta, aged a minimum of 28 days. Fresh halibut is pan-roasted, splashed with a tomato fennel broth, served with risotto. There's blackened Atlantic salmon served on a bed of wasabi-spiked potatoes with a sake-laced cream. Solid wine list, shareworthy desserts.

Madrina's Ristorante

$$

20 Balsam Avenue   (403) 949-2750 R

Open Tuesday–Sunday 11:30 AM–3:00 PM, 5:30 AM–10:00 PM

V, MC, DEBIT

> A series of decks nestled under the pines greets diners at Madrina's. This restaurant is all about classic Italian cooking with a few pizzas thrown in for good measure. Try the scampi (not shrimp) grilled and served with simple lemon butter. Prawns are sautéed, finished with brandy and fresh lime juice, napped with a creamy red curry sauce. The filetto Rossini is grilled tenderloin with crisp curls of pancetta, and a Gorgonzola sauce with demi-glace. The handsome interior with twinkling white lights is celebratory and romantic.

◉ PRIDDIS

The Priddis Greens Golf Club

$$

1 Priddis Greens Drive   (403) 931-3171 R

Open daily summer 8:00 AM–9:00 PM

Open winter Friday 5:00 AM–9:00 PM; Saturday 11:00 AM–9:00 PM

Sunday brunch 10:30 AM–1:00 PM

V, MC, AE

> It's an exceptional brunch, well worth the scenic drive from Calgary or Bragg Creek. Chef Nicolas Desinai buys his lamb from a local sheep farmer, and uses as many regional products as possible. The carvery—roast lamb, ham, turkey—is a bountiful feast and changes weekly.

The View and Brew

$

Priddis Plaza   (403) 931-3611

Open Monday–Thursday 7:30 AM–7:00 PM

Friday 7:30 AM–8:00 PM

Saturday 8:00 AM–7:00 PM; Sunday 9:00 AM–7:00 PM

V, MC, DEBIT

> Walk through the gift shop to the back, where you'll find a comfortable deli-style café that serves whatever you see in the glass-front counter. Casseroles, mac and cheese with real cheddar, homemade cakes and delicious scratch pies. Good spot for a light lunch or tea.
>
> Take some time to check out Collatio, a luxe shop next door filled with objets d'art for home and body.

$$ **Café Divine**

42 McCrae Street   (403) 938-0000

Open summer Monday 11:00 AM–2:30 PM

Tuesday–Saturday 11:00 AM–2:30 PM, 5:30 PM–9:00 PM

Open winter Tuesday–Saturday 11:00 AM–2:30 PM, 5:30 PM–9:00 PM

V, MC, DEBIT

> Darren Nixon and Adrienne Penny run a bright, busy dining room with an open kitchen and a small deli counter. The menu changes often, and it might include braised short ribs in merlot sauce with saskatoons, Alberta lamb shanks braised in red wine with aromatic spices, or grilled lamb loin with raspberry sauce and black pepper crème fraîche. The daily soup is made with fresh stock, and local vegetables and Alberta lamb are favourite ingredients. Darren smokes his own salmon—try it with maple cream cheese on sourdough. Excellent house-made breads and lots of calorific desserts.

Hansel and Gretel Meats

49 Elizabeth Street   (403) 938-4400

Open Monday–Saturday 9:00 AM–5:00 PM

V, MC, DEBIT

> Harry Wietele is a fifth-generation sausage maker. He and his wife, Martina, own and operate this busy meat market/deli/lunch spot. Sausage is his art—bratwurst, Polish, Hungarian, pepperoni, fresh farmers' sausage, and cold cuts of all kinds, as well as a few cheeses, pickles and other deli items.
>
> There are twenty seats for lunch. Choose among four different soups, hearty sandwiches and hot lunch items such as beef stew or schnitzel, all house made. Harry's long experience as head chef at Spruce Meadows has made him an expert in off-site catering, and the Wieteles have developed a thriving event business.

The Saskatoon Farm   www.saskatoonfarm.com

near Okotoks   (403) 938-6245

Café open daily 9:00 AM–5:00 PM

> The farm is a happy combination of café, greenhouse and garden centre with old-timey storefront shops. It's not far from the Sheep River, a bit north of Aldersyde, a bit south of Okotoks.
>
> Paul Hamer's Saskatoon Farm began as a barley field, but now it's a prolific small fruit orchard, mostly saskatoons and sour cherries. He also raises a herd of

Café Divine's Braised Lamb Shanks
with Ginger, Merlot and Saskatoons

Chef Darren Nixon of Café Divine in Okotoks makes braised lamb shanks with saskatoons and merlot. He serves it with mascarpone potatoes. We think it's divine, and
even better when made a day ahead. Serves 4

4 lamb shanks, fat trimmed
salt and pepper
2 shallots, finely sliced
2 slices fresh ginger, julienned
1 cup saskatoons, fresh or frozen
1 cup merlot wine
¼ cup liquid honey
1 cup chicken stock
1 teaspoon chile flakes

Place lamb shanks in a deep pan that can be covered. Salt and pepper them. Roast at
450°F, uncovered, until well browned, about 30 minutes.

Add remaining ingredients. Cover. Reduce oven to 350°F and braise about two
hours, or until meat comes easily from the bone. Remove shanks, strain sauce, and
serve shanks with sauce and potatoes. NOTE: For a perfect sauce, strain the juices;
chill until fat rises and is easily removed. Reheat the shanks in the de-fatted sauce
and serve with mascarpone potatoes.

Mascarpone Mashed Potatoes

6 large russet potatoes, peeled
½ cup (125 mL) mascarpone cheese
½ cup (125 mL) cream
1 tablespoon (15 mL) butter
salt and white pepper

Boil potatoes until soft. Put through a ricer, or mash by hand. Using a large spoon,
gradually beat in cheese, cream and butter. Potatoes will be soft and creamy. Finish
with salt and white pepper. We'd rather eat these than ice cream. Serves 4

bison, and between the bison main courses and the saskatoon desserts, the menu in his café takes on a distinctly Canadian flavour.

Look for bison meat in the burritos, the burgers and the smokies. Try delicious white-chocolate saskatoon scones. For many people, the highlight is a piece of genuine saskatoon pie, topped off with saskatoon white-chocolate ripple ice cream.

Hamar has worked with a Calgary microbrewery, the Brew Brothers, to produce a saskatoon beer, and you can buy saskatoon lemonade in the café.

"We serve great chili," says Hamer. "And we make a fruit cake better than anything I've ever tasted. None of those funny green things in it—just saskatoons and sour cherries."

From Calgary, head south 19 km on Hwy 2; go east (left) on 338 Avenue (look for signage); continue east for 3 km. Road dead-ends at the farm.

Saskatoon Brunch Pudding

Saskatoons are grown on more than 100 U-Pick operations throughout Alberta. The Food Lovers think their deep colour and rich, winey flavour is a taste of heaven. We made this with saskatoons from the Coronado Saskatoon Farm north of Gibbons. But we've also made it with raspberries from Roy's Raspberries, a U-Pick east of Edmonton.

2 cups (500 mL) day-old bread cubes
2 cups (500 mL) 2% milk
2 tablespoons (30 mL) melted butter
3 eggs
¼ cup (50 mL) sugar
1 teaspoon (5 mL) vanilla
½ teaspoon (1 mL) salt
1 cup (250) saskatoons, fresh or frozen

Put bread cubes in a buttered 8-inch round baking dish. Slightly beat milk, butter, eggs, sugar, vanilla and salt together and pour over bread cubes. Fold in saskatoons. Cover and refrigerate overnight.

Remove from fridge 20 minutes before baking. Put casserole in a cake pan and pour boiling water into the pan. Bake pudding, uncovered, at 350°F (180°C) for 45 minutes, or until set. Let the pudding rest 10 minutes before serving. Serves 6.

$

Evelyn's Memory Lane Café

118 4th Avenue SW   (403) 652-1887

Open Monday–Friday 9:00 AM–7:00 PM

Saturday 11:00 AM–7:00 PM; Sunday 12:00 PM–6:00 PM

DEBIT

Don and Evelyn Zabloski's place is another in the spate of 1950s diners that have popped up all over the province. They have forty-three seats including the counter, and Don's electric train runs around the ceiling, its authentic whistle hooting merrily. This diner is unique because Eveyln is a stickler for quality. Ice cream, for instance. They buy their 12 per cent cream from Foothills Dairy and make many flavours from scratch, like the rhubarb white chocolate made with local rhubarb, and the saskatoon ripple with fruit from the Saskatoon Farm. Exotic flavours aside, the most popular is still vanilla. "We use pure Madagascar vanilla," she says.

Evelyn Zabloski

When Evelyn Zablonski lived in Banff, she owned and operated Evelyn's Coffee Bar, and a second coffee bar and café, Evelyn's II, with a little more of the same thing: good coffee and great, simple food. Her chocolate cake, cinnamon buns and roast chicken sandwiches were nationally famous. Inevitably, someone made her an offer she couldn't refuse.

"I was tired," she says. "Banff was incredibly busy—we worked almost 24 hours a day. I needed a change."

After looking around for a spot to roost, Evelyn and her husband Don ended up in the pretty southern town of High River, a tad slower-paced than Banff, yet still close enough to the Rockies to feel like home.

"We found this old-fashioned ice cream store, and it felt right."

They call it Evelyn's Memory Lane Café, and compared to the frenetic pace of running two shops in the busiest resort in the Rockies, this sounds like a walk in the park. Not so, says Evelyn. It's smaller, a little quieter, but High River is definitely a happening town, and when she's not baking and cooking, she's learning more about the ice cream business.

"I want to go to that big ice cream convention in Florida," she says. "Just as soon as I have time."

Evelyn's roast chicken sandwich is legendary. Other hot lunches include casseroles, scratch soups daily and a terrific hot roast beef sandwich. Try the broccoli yogurt salad, the cinnamon buns when available and the house-made pastries and desserts.

◎ TURNER VALLEY

Coyote Moon Cantina and Espresso Bar

202 Main Street   (403) 933-3363

Open Sunday 8:00 AM–5:00 PM; Monday, Tuesday 7:00 AM–6:00 PM

Wednesday–Saturday 7:00 AM–8:00 PM

V, MC, DEBIT

They make a good organic granola in this funky 80-year-old building. Other breakfast goodies include French toast and the Coyote steak breakfast with two eggs, pan-fries and toast. After that it's the usual lunch—sandwiches, house-made chili and soups, lots of choice in wraps. Owner Maureen Janssen's desserts—pies, carrot or chocolate zucchini cake and fruit crisps—are her own. Her favourite thing is quiche, but it's not always available. Specialty coffees, Italian sodas, milkshakes, and they do a mean banana split. Ask for it. Licensed.

◎ BLACK DIAMOND

The Black Diamond Hotel boasts what may be the longest bar in Alberta. Worth a look, and if you want a beer and pizza, it can be a lively spot on a Saturday night.

The Stop

123 Government Road   (403) 933-3002

Open Sunday–Thursday 7:00 AM–10:00 PM; Friday, Saturday 7:00 AM–11:00 PM

CASH ONLY

Mike Kingston's place is an internet café, coffee house, and local venue for rubber-chicken-throwing contests. All summer long Thursday night is cook-your-own-steak night, and he likes to grill Spolumbo sausages on the barbie. Food is more casual in winter. Big treat? His homemade chocolate oat coconut macaroons. Live entertainment—jazz or blues—on a semi-regular basis.

Mike's Chocolate Coconut Macaroons

2 cups (500 mL) granulated sugar
6 tablespoons (90 mL) cocoa
½ cup (125 mL) butter
½ cup (125 mL) milk
2 cups (500 mL) quick oats
2 cups (500 mL) shredded coconut

Place sugar, cocoa, butter and milk in a pan. Bring to a boil for one minute. Remove from heat and stir in rolled oats and coconut—mixture will be thick. Spoon onto waxed paper by tablespoons, flattening slightly. Cool and store in an airtight container. Mike likes to freeze these.

$ **Wonders Coffee House**

130 Government Street (403) 933-2347

Open daily 6:30 AM–10:00 PM

V, MC, DEBIT

> An old-timey spot for specialty coffees and desserts. It's part café, part gift shop and part tourist information bureau, and browsers seem to be welcome. Watch for the porch with billowing flower baskets in the summer. In winter it's a cozy retreat.

$ **Marv's Classic Soda Shop**

121 Centre Street (403) 933-7001

Open daily winter 10:00 AM–5:30 PM

Open daily summer 10:00 AM–9:00 PM

MC, DEBIT

> Marv's place has been used for several movies, and when you see it you'll know why. The working soda fountain comes with all the memorabilia from the '40s and '50s, plus good milkshakes made with real ice cream, and burgers, including the famous peanut butter burger. They sell traditional penny candy, and the place is stuffed with antiques, including a functioning jukebox.

$$ **Route 40 Soup Company**

126 Centre Street   (403) 933-7676 R

Open Monday–Friday 8:00 AM–9:00 PM; Friday, Saturday 9:00 AM–8:00 PM

V, MC, DEBIT

> Now we're into serious cooking. This tiny restaurant (four tables, two seats at the counter) is the kind of place we always hope to stumble upon, and seldom do. The menu changes with whatever the chef brings in, and dinner is truly a culinary journey. The night we were there it started with organic greens, bocconcini cheese and fresh-picked tomatoes from Whiskey Creek. The main course was organic free-range chicken breast with Italian sausage, sundried tomatoes, fresh basil and three cheeses, served on herbed linguini. For dessert, there was frozen Callebaut mousse cake on a blueberry maple compote, finished off with a chocolate-dipped almond wafer. Breakfasts involve Spolumbo's sausage and eggs with spinach, tomatoes and pancetta in a wrap, pancakes with a bumbleberry mixture, eggs and sausages from A7 Ranche Natural Sausages, or owner Lanny Klaudt's own muffins with fresh fruit. Lunch is equally toothsome—try the five spice pork loin with Route 40 sweet apricot chutney and homemade relish. It comes in a wrap, with Route 40 homefries—sweet potato, Yukon gold, and blue potatoes, with two homemade dips. Or try the Thai salad—romaine, steam-fried noodles, Thai lime dressing topped with red onions, fresh Thai basil and toasted almonds.

LONGVIEW

Deep in cowboy country is Longview, not far from the Highwood River, the Chain Lakes, the historic Bar U ranch (open late May through early October) and Kananaskis Country.

$$ **Longview Steakhouse**

102 Morrison Road (Hwy 22)   (403) 558-2000

Open summer Tuesday–Sunday 8:00 AM–9:00 PM

Open winter Wednesday–Sunday 8:00 AM–9:00 PM

V, MC

> Walk into the Longview, and you know by the cowboy hats and singular cut of the customers' jib that you're in cowboy country. The owners, who formerly worked for Chateaubriand in Calgary, run a real western steakhouse with a local clientele and the best beef. There are other choices—chicken, ribs, seafood—but the

steaks are triple-A, tender and accurately grilled. The desserts are house-made, including a delicious cheesecake.

$ **Black Cat Swiss Restaurant**
108 Morrison Road (Hwy 22)   (403) 558-0000
Open Thursday–Tuesday 12:00 PM–9:00 PM
V, MC, DEBIT

> When we visited the Black Cat, the only animal in sight was the Belmoufid family's much-loved black dog. This is Swiss cooking, with homemade soups, traditional sauces, plate-filling schnitzel and bratwurst, served with tender spaetzle or rosti.

$ **Ian's Navajo Mug**
140 Morrison Road (Hwy 22)   (403) 558-2272
Open Monday, Wednesday 9:00 AM–7:00 PM
Tuesday 11:00 AM–7:00 PM; Thursday–Sunday 9:00 AM–9:00 PM
V, MC, DEBIT

> They make a good cuppa java here, and you can have sandwiches, cookies or muffins, but it's also a souvenir shop, and tourists come here on the off chance that co-owner Ian Tyson might drop by and autograph a CD. Singer-songwriter Tyson ranches just outside Longview.

$ **Heidi's Food Saloon**
110 Morrison Road (Hwy 22)   (403) 558-2008
Open daily 6:00 AM–3:00 PM
V, MC, AE, DEBIT

> Heidi Herrmann speaks German, and cooks a darn fine breakfast. It's not the longest menu in town, but she also does lunches—soups and sandwiches.

Longview Jerky Shop
Open Monday–Friday 8:00 AM–7:00 PM   (403) 558-3960
Saturday, Sunday 9:00 AM–7:00 PM
V, MC, AE, DEBIT

> Back in 1979 the Longview Jerky Shop opened its doors, and they haven't looked back. On offer is locally raised Alberta beef, dried and cured by an old recipe, and available in several flavours, including honey garlic, teriyaki, sweet n' spicy, peppered and original. They also produce a pioneer-style jerky, available double-smoked. Jerky stix, a new product last year, uses bison, pork and beef, and

produces a tender, easy-chewing jerky. Local hunters make use of the Longview for custom cutting their own wild game.

◎ COWLEY

Back Country Butchering

508 Railway Avenue   (403) 628-2686

Open Monday–Friday 9:00 AM–5:00 PM; Saturday 9:00 AM–3:00 PM

V, MC, AE DEBIT

There are a lot of hunters living in these hills, and Tim Ewing and Doug Ross have turned their meat-cutting skills into an essential service here in the high country. Last year they processed 350 elk, 400 deer and 60 moose, and made 30,000 pounds of game sausage. House specialties include many varieties of sausages, smokies or jerkies—try the maple jerky stick. They age the meat up to five weeks before cutting it. Bestsellers are prime rib steaks and finger ribs for barbecue. On a Saturday morning, they'll sell 60 or 70 marinated steaks. If you have a big

appetite and a freezer, beef is available by the sides, front or hind quarters. "We advertise when it's local." There's also a good selection of specialty condiments here, including Bustard's Mustards from Pincher Creek and Pepperheads Hot Sauces from Turner Valley.

◎ PINCHER CREEK

Denise's Bistro

732 Kettles Street   (403) 627-1875

Open Tuesday–Saturday 9:00 AM–9:00 PM

V, MC, DEBIT

Denise's Bistro holds about two dozen people seated, plus a lineup at the counter waiting for takeout. We like the ever-changing lunches and the decadent desserts.

Denise is noted for her international dinner menus. Huge sandwiches, good, fresh salads and we especially recommend the corn chicken chowder, a thick, flavour-packed bowl with ample chicken, carrots, onion, other vegetables, and in season, local corn.

Bridges Natural Foods
756 Kettles Street   (403) 627-3767
Open Monday–Saturday 9:00 AM–6:00 PM
V, MC

A good spot to stock up on organic beans and grains, pasta and nut butters. They also have a small deli selection of organic beef and turkey, etc., plus a produce section and some healthy baked goods.

◉ TWIN BUTTE

$ **Country General Store and Restaurant**
Hwy 6 between Pincher Creek and Waterton Gate   (403) 627-4035
Open daily summer 10:00 AM–8:00 PM
Open winter Monday 10:00 AM–3:00 PM; Wednesday–Sunday 10:00 AM–8:00 PM
V, MC, AE, DEBIT

If you whiz past this little white store with the red trim, you'll be missing a treat. The country store/gift shop/post office includes a small gallery in the back room and a sizeable café with some pretty good Mexican food served all day long— huevos rancheros, quesadillas, taco or enchilada combination plates, burritos. Clint and Jeny Davis serve western food too: bison burgers, elk burgers, beef

burgers, well-dressed pizzas, and even a kids' menu. The beer is cold, there's entertainment some weekends, and there's a huge community table, Santa Fe-style, so you can sit down for dinner and converse with a perfect stranger, or even an imperfect one, which is usually more fun anyway. You could have an ice cream cone on the way out.

◎ WATERTON

Prince of Wales Hotel

$$ (left margin)

774 Railroad Street   (403) 859-2231
Open daily summer 11:00 AM–10:00 PM
V, MC, AE, DEBIT

It's a massive old pile of a lodge perched on a windblown hill. In the lobby tea room, you can indulge in a proper high tea and watch an occasional storm blowing up the valley, ruffling the lake.

We actually prefer the Windsor Lounge next door, a civilized pub with a fireplace, the same exquisite view, a short, well-stocked bar and a piano. Best bets are a selection of charcuterie with assorted cheeses, or a true Alberta specialty: beef and buffalo carpaccio with a drizzle of olive oil and a good grinding of black pepper.

Across the lobby, the Royal Stewart Dining Room (note the spiffy tartans on the staff) looks more like an upscale summer camp, and the food is a bit more relaxed than the grand hotel style this place once served. Try the cinnamon roasted loin of pork with apple chutney, or the juicy shepherd's pie with its fluffy mashed potato topping, and accompany it with a Sleeman's amber ale. Someone has selected appropriate and interesting beers to pair with main courses, which we think is a great idea.

Lamp Post Dining Room

Kilmorey Lodge, 117 Evergreen Avenue   (403) 859-2334 R
Open daily summer 7:30 AM–10:00 PM; Open daily winter 8:00 AM–9:00 PM

For the second year in a row, our waitress didn't have a clue what the chef's name was, but whoever he may be (they do know it's a man), we applaud his efforts to use some regional ingredients. Good solid breakfasts here, with real oatmeal and house-made granola as well as the usual egg dishes. For dinner try the delicious wild game chili, the grilled elk chop with sauce Bordelaise, or the striploin of bison. The chef glazes pork roast with maple syrup, and the salmon is cedar-planked. There's a toothsome dish of wild mushrooms in a stroganoff-style sour cream sauce. For dessert, there's saskatoon pie. The wine list has real strength in VQA choices, always a good thing to see. The Lamp Post is their major dining room, but there's also a cozy lounge directly off the lobby, and many people prefer to eat there.

Waterton Peaks Café

303 Windflower Avenue   (403) 859-2144

Open daily May–September 11:00 AM–10:00 PM

V, MC, DEBIT

It's rare to find a little gem like the Peaks Café in a resort town. Greg and Adriana Vogt own this café. The menu changes constantly, but it's all in-house—soups, breads, salads, sandwiches, muffins, cookies—comfort food with an edge. When we were there, the chef was baking pizza-like Italian flatbreads with sundried tomatoes, artichoke hearts and pesto. At dinner the pièce de résistance is the chicken breast stuffed with blue cheese and fresh tarragon, served with house potatoes.

We love the use of local, seasonal ingredients in their splendid desserts —the strawberry pie, the fresh strawberry crisp with real whipped cream, the rhubarb coffee cake served with two sauces—a sweet rhubarb sauce and a maple custard sauce. The rhubarb dream square has a buttery shortbread base and a fresh rhubarb topping with maple custard sauce, the plate artfully dappled with rhubarb juice and freshly chopped

The Peaks Rhubarb Dream Cake

Crust:

2 cups flour

2/3 cup icing sugar

1 cup butter

Cut butter into sugar and flour until fine. Pat into a 9 x 13 pan. Bake at 350°F, 15 minutes, just until edges are golden brown.

Filling:

4 eggs

3 cups sugar

1 cup flour

5 cups diced red rhubarb

Beat eggs and 2 cups sugar until thick and golden. Beat in 3 cup flour. Fold in rhubarb. Pour over baked crust. Stir together 1 cup sugar and 3 cup flour. Sprinkle over rhubarb mixture. Return to oven and bake 45 minutes at 350°F. Serve with maple custard sauce.

mint leaves. The ginger cake with fresh ginger whipped cream is as good as the fresh apple pie and the oat-walnut brownie with whipped cream and raspberries. They'll pack a hiker's lunch that will make all the huffing and puffing worthwhile. In the off-season, Greg cooks at the well-regarded Aerie Resort on Vancouver Island.

Ye Olde Lick and Nibble
Windflower Avenue
Seasonal
CASH

Surely the smallest shop in Waterton, they do a huge business in ice cream—all the traditional flavours from Foothills Creamery, plus some unusual ones, including saskatoon. Oh, bewildering choice. Torn between pralines and cream and tiger tiger? Undecided customers can have a sample or two—just enough for a lick (or a nibble?) to help make up your mind.

Welch's Candy Store and Coffee Shop
Windflower Avenue   (403) 859-2363
Open daily summer 7:00 AM–10:00 PM
V, MC, DEBIT

Ice cream for breakfast? This is the place. The shop offers ice cream in all the flavours, their own frozen yogurt, house-made fudge, penny candy, jawbreakers, licorice and European chocolate bars. Carol Robbins' sister Paulette owns the Welch's in Banff (403) 762-3737 (V1 p. 64).

FROM VOLUME ONE WE STILL LIKE
The HQ Pie Shop in Cochrane (403) 932-2111 (p. 5); Mountain Bistro and Pizzeria, Bragg Creek (403) 949-3800 (p. 7); La P'tite Table, Okotoks (403) 938-2224 (p. 6); Black Diamond Bakery, Black Diamond (403) 933-4503 (p. 4); Memories Inn, Longview, (403) 558-3665 (p. 6); High Country Café, Millarville (403) 931-3866 (p. 5); Millarville Farmers Market (403) 931-3866 (p. 225)

crowsnest
◎   COLEMAN
We're in the Crowsnest Pass, an area steeped in a history that includes bootleggers, rum runners, gold miners and coal miners, and the natural disaster of 1903 we know as the Frank Slide. The slide took 70 lives. Just eleven years later the Hillcrest Mine would suffer a massive underground explosion, taking the lives of 189 coal miners. Today it's pos-

sible to tour an original tunnel in the coal mine at Bellevue, and visit the Frank Slide Interpretive Centre in the town of Frank or the excellent Crowsnest Museum in Coleman. In the Crowsnest, expect hearty food, friendly people and the rugged beauty of small hard-working towns within the footprint of the Rocky Mountains.

$ **Chris's Restaurant**
7802 17th Avenue   (403) 563-3093
Open Monday–Saturday 8:00 AM–9:00 PM; Sunday 8:00 AM–4:00 PM
V, MC

> "It used to be Chris and Irwin's place. Irwin passed years ago, they just haven't changed the sign," says our helpful waitress, who also advises that the pancakes are huge, and the ham steak is too. The coal miner's breakfast has been served here since 1975, when miners coming off shift would need breakfast in the afternoon. The mines have closed, but the café has staying power, and locals still eat here. The "egg cetera" section of the menu offers eggs any style with steak, or with toast. There are the huge pancakes, the thick-cut French toast, the slab of ham, the crispy bacon and the bottomless coffee is frequently topped up. If you aren't in the mood for breakfast, try a burger or the cabbage rolls—it's all homemade.

$$ **Popiel's**
Highway 3, in town   (403) 563-5555
Open Monday–Saturday 8:00 AM–9:30 PM; Sunday 8:00 AM–9:00 PM
V, MC, AE, DEBIT

> An extensive menu: breakfast, lunch and dinner, specials for kids and seniors. Try the Kananaskis burger with horseradish, or the yakisoba kengo—noodles, Japanese style, with a stir-fry of pork or chicken. The cabbage rolls are meat-stuffed, the liver comes with bacon and onions, or they'll make you a pizza. The big fancy dinner is the Popiel's platter for two—lobster, shrimp, scallops, clams and calamari.

$$ **Rum Runner**
7902 20th Avenue   (403) 562-7552
Open daily 11:00 AM–11:00 PM
V, MC, DEBIT

> Formerly Pic's Roadhouse, this busy restaurant and pub beside the Holy Crow Bar serves wings, burgers, ribs and a pretty good steak. The Rum Runner is located in a historic open-beam building with an amazing bar, once a prop for the movie Showboat. In summer, the patio offers a gorgeous view of the surrounding mountains.

The Cinnamon Bear Bakery and Café
8342B 20th Avenue (Main Street)   (403) 562-2443
Open daily 8:00 AM–6:00 PM

It's a bright, busy café and gift shop with the smell of bake-off sweet doughs and good coffee. They also do Belgian waffles, soups, sandwiches and chili. Try the cinnamon bear's claw and coffee for a takeaway breakfast. It's convenient.

Mountain Bakery
12849 20th Avenue (Main Street)
(403) 562-7999
Open Monday–Saturday 9:00 AM–6:00 PM
DEBIT

Jean-Bernard Gauthier is from the Val de Loire, in France, and he bakes a most delicious loaf of bread, with a chewy crust, an interior the colour of old ivory, and an open, airy structure (the crumb). Nothing in this bread but flour, yeast, salt and water, and a slow, cool rise. No fat, no preservatives. Go early and buy it still warm. He also does some fancy patisserie work like profiteroles and cookies that look inviting, but we'll go back for the bread.

Stone's Throw Café
13047 20th Avenue (Main Street)   (403) 562-2230
Open daily 6:30 AM–6:00 PM
DEBIT

Good spot for a quick early breakfast—plain coffee or espresso, big homemade muffins and cinnamon buns. They also do light lunches: soup, salads, sandwiches. We love the cheese and onion scone. We also love the Rivers Edge Log Works, next door, where we bought exquisite pottery and lovely one-of-a-kind tableware.

$$ **Bistro on Main**

13019 20th Avenue (Main Street)   (403) 563-3333

Open Tuesday–Thursday 11:00 AM–10:00 PM

Friday, Saturday 11:00 AM–11:00 PM

V, MC, DEBIT

> Peter and Janet Joy have the classiest dining room in town, with an eclectic menu
> offering everything from crab cakes with jalapeno jelly, and curry samosas with
> mango yogurt, to apricot-stuffed pork tenderloin, pan-fried stuffed Rocky
> Mountain trout and roasted rack of lamb. Lots of tapas-style items, along with six
> pizzas and salads made with organic greens. Hearty sandwiches and wraps.

◉ B E L L E V U E

The Old Dairy Ice Cream Shoppe

Main Street   (403) 564-4111

Seasonal May–September

CASH

> Open over 40 years, this summer-only ice cream shop offers the best of Nestle,
> Breyers and Foothills, with both soft and hard ice creams. The soft ice cream
> comes in 20 flavours, including English toffee.

$$ **Moose Mountain Grill**

21508 27th Avenue   (403) 562-8999 R

Open summer Thursday–Monday 11:00 AM–11:00 PM

Open winter Monday, Thursday, Friday 5:00 PM–11:00 PM; Saturday 5:00 PM–11:00 PM

V, MC, DEBIT

> Owner Carol Ann Smith whizzes around her old Craftsman-style house (original
> half-pillars, still-shiny linoleum), delivering plates of tasty home-cooked food.
> It's a small but ambitious menu, with items like pork marsala and some basic,
> well-executed comfort food (the mac and cheese). For dessert there's a superb
> chocolate lava cake served warm, the molten chocolate centre running a little
> when you cut into it. This place is often booked for special dinners, and the chef
> does some cooking classes.

◎ RAYMOND

The Old Country Sausage Shop
Between the golf course and the hospital   (403) 752-3006

> Long owned by Klaus and Mary Lee Schumann, this sausage shop, also known as Raymond Meats, operates on old-world recipes. Klaus uses no fillers or MSG, and his naturally-smoked sausages have won him a passel of awards. Artisan meat shops like this one are becoming a rarity.

Raymond Burger Baron and Pizza
189 Broadway Street N   (403) 752-3747
(Intersection, Main Street and Hwy 52)
Open Monday–Thursday 11:00 AM–9:00 PM; Friday, Saturday 11:00 AM–10:00 PM
Sunday 11:00 AM–8:00 PM; Closed Sunday in winter
V, MC, DEBIT

> Since 1990, this independent burger and pizza joint has been operated by the Najjar family, Nadim and Eva, and it's a favourite stop for travellers from all over the south country. Nadim is a stickler for quality beef, and Eva makes all the sauces herself. The Raymond burger is their house specialty, and Omar's burger, double or triple with special mushroom sauce, is a popular choice.

Bloomin' Inn
7 km west of Pincher Creek on Tower Road   www.bloomin-inn.com
Open daily 10:00 am–4:00 pm   (403) 627-5829
v, mc, debit

> The Cyrs, Francois and Colleen along with their daughter Jenny, have opened a food store on their property selling their farm raised natural beef, lamb, fowl, buffalo and pork. There's a picnic area, farm tours by arrangement and their ranch-style B&B.

It's easy to like this bustling southern city, with its broad, tree-lined streets, gracious old homes, and vibrant cultural mix. This year we found a couple of exciting new places. For some fortuitous reason, a single block of turn-of-the-century buildings on 2nd Avenue at 4th Street maintains the flavour of old Asia. A couple of stores and eateries here have roots that run deep in the Lethbridge community.

O-Sho Japanese Restaurant

$

311 4th Street S   (403) 327-8382

Open Monday–Friday 11:30 AM–2:30 PM

Monday–Saturday 4:00 PM–10:00 PM

Sunday and holidays 4:00 PM–9:00 PM

V, MC, AE

> The Japanese presence has been an important part of Lethbridge history, and O-Sho brings a taste of traditional favourites westerners have come to love. Along with the standards—the yakitori, tempura, gyoza, noodle dishes and the deep-fried breaded (katsu) dishes everybody loves, they offer a few more unusual items. Try the edamame, if available—fresh green soybeans, salted. A good sushi menu boasts nigiri sushi, sashimi (try the O-Sho boat or the love boat combos) and a big selection of norimaki. Maki dishes include some originals, like the Kentucky maki and the sweet Japanese mushroom maki. Try the house special maki, a combo of scallop, prawn, tuna, salmon roe and avocado. Combination dinners are available for one or two. Two sushi chefs, kimono-clad waitresses and a bright, clean look round out this place.

Nakagama's Japanese Food and Gifts

322 2nd Avenue S   (403) 327-5337

Open Monday–Friday 9:00 AM–6:00 PM

Saturday 9:00 AM–5:30 PM

V, MC

> Ken Nakagama's corner shop carries every authentic Japanese ingredient you could want, from marinades to pickled ginger and pristine fish for sushi. Every Wednesday he makes his special ling cod cake; on Fridays and Saturdays he offers take-away sushi.
>
> The shop also carries essentials for table setting—chopsticks, attractive paper goods, lovely hand-painted bowls and serving pieces, bento boxes, lacquerware and ceramics, sake sets and tea sets.

Bow On Tong Co.

316 2nd Avenue S   (403) 327-3675

Open most afternoons 2:00 PM–5:00 PM

The same family has owned this unusual shop for more than 100 years, and the owner, Albert Leung, lives in the back. His shop is beautiful—almost a living museum, filled with exquisite Chinese basketry, and Albert is a fount of information on the history of the place. Notice the magnificent old Chinese medicinal chest with its many diminutive drawers and, without a doubt, a few secret compartments. Alas, there's no longer a resident herbalist. Note the Chinese Opera Society in this building, across the street from the Chinese National League.

Or-Kids Organics

314 2nd Avenue S   (403) 327-7736

Open Monday–Saturday 10:00 AM–6:00 PM

V, MC, AE, DEBIT

Roger and Sherry Bruinsma started this shop with healthy baking for kids—the peanut butter cookie had flax, rosehips and alfalfa, but tasted kid-friendly. They've expanded into a full service organic grocery with fresh local produce in season, frozen meats, local organic dairy from Fairwinds Farms. Their certified organic beef comes from Guitton's near Claresholm, and the buffalo is from Windy Ridge Ranch.

Tongue'n Groove

312 2nd Avenue S   (403) 320-7074

Monday–Saturday 3:00 PM–3:00 AM; Sunday 6:00 PM–3:00 AM

V, MC

A dark, atmospheric little bar with red paper lanterns and cool music. This is the centre of the new Canadian music scene in Lethbridge. Sunday is open stage, and on the last Wednesday of every month is Most Vocal Poet Troupe, the spoken word event. Wines are supplied by Andrew Hilton Wine Merchants and you can get a selection of single malts scotch. Word has it that the basement was a warren of long-ago opium dens. Casual munchie-type food—hummus, soups, sandwiches.

La Bella Notte

Fire Hall #1, 402 2nd Avenue S   (403) 331-3319 R

Open Monday–Saturday 11:30 AM–2:00 PM, 4:30 PM–10:30 PM; Sunday 4:30 PM–9:30 PM

V, MC, AE, DEBIT

What a wonderful use for an old fire hall. We love the way the Lagunas family has turned this intimidating space into an intimate dining room with stunning decor.

The part you don't see? Fresh herbs growing on the roof, which, by the way, has a great view of Lethbridge. The menu is extensive, the cooking classic, almost retro. You might want to start with sliced portobello mushrooms sautéed with garlic, fresh herbs, balsamic vinegar and white wine, or a house-made pasta, served here as a main course, including an oven-baked cheese stuffed ravioli in a four-cheese cream sauce. Mains are garlic-marinated grilled lamb, several seafood dishes, veal-stuffed tortellini in a vodka sauce, and gnocchi in a spicy marinara (red) sauce, topped with chicken breast and sautéed mussels. There are separate menu sections for veal, beef, chicken and additional seafood dishes. The wine list is strong in Italian and Australian choices, but has only two from Canada, both VQA.

$ **Choices Café**
100 5th Street S   (403) 329-8888
Open Monday–Saturday 11:00 AM–10:00 PM
V, MC, DEBIT

> And choices you shall have, dozens of them. There's an extensive menu of appetizers, salads, sandwiches, wraps, pasta and pizza, plus 16 entrees that come with a choice of over 20 sides. The chef uses organic chicken, natural Galloway range-fed beef, wild salmon (one of a handful of restaurants that bother to distinguish between wild and farmed). Need a gluten-free pizza? They'll make one with a high-protein wheat-free crust. We like the Santa Monica fried salad with roasted veggies and organic romaine, the house-smoked beef, the toga wrap (lots of fresh vegetables, feta cheese, balsamic vinaigrette and pork tenderloin). We also admire their commitment to a definite food philosophy and regional/local ingredients. It's a big, friendly restaurant on the corner with a small summer patio out front, but on a Friday night the place was almost empty. We hope there's enough local support to keep this business afloat.

$ **Esquires Coffee and Internet Café**
621 4th Avenue S   (403) 380-6747
Open Monday–Saturday 7:00 AM–10:00 PM; Sunday 11:00 AM–5:00 PM
V, DEBIT

> We don't usually include chains in the Food Lover's Trail Guide, but doggone it,

this place just had to be in the book. It was one of two great cups of coffee we found in Lethbridge, the other being at The Penny Coffee House (V1 p. 181). We liked the friendly, obliging service, the sleek uptown decor in the majestic former Royal Bank, and the convenience of the internet in clean, attractive surroundings. (Why do so many internet cafés look like they need to be scrubbed down?)

Broxburn Vegetables and Café

4.6 km east of Lethbridge, 1 km south on Broxburn Road   (403) 327-0909
Open March–December Monday–Saturday 9:00 AM–4:00 PM; lunch 11:00 AM–3:00 PM
V, MC, AE, DEBIT

Owner Paul de Jonge and his chef, Jarrod Gigliotti (formerly of CoCo Pazzo) are operating a little gem in the country, provisioning the kitchen from their prolific U-Pick gardens.

Stop by for pie and coffee, or have the whole meal deal—roasted red pepper soup served with an Alberta beef steak sandwich, or garden salads with their own vegetables. Their signature dish? The famous broxberry pie made with strawberries, raspberries, red currants, black currants and saskatoons from their gardens. The dining room can seat 60, the verandah another 50. Note: Most people buy vegetables on the way home—the veggie store is cash only.

FROM VOLUME ONE WE STILL LIKE

Coco Pazzo, (403)329-8979 (p. 181); Penny Coffee House, (403) 320-5282 (p. 181); Saigonese, (403) 327-7225 (p. 182)

Driving from Lethbridge to Taber with the windows down, you can smell raw potato starch in the air, followed by the distinct aroma of frying potatoes. McCain's and Lamb Weston both operate big processing plants here, where potato fields are as common as cornfields in Taber.

Ernie's Whole Hog Mobile Roastery   (403) 223-8018

How festive is this? Ernie and Miriam Waldner will run their mobile pork roastery right up to your door and roast a whole hog for your party. Talk about impressing the neighbours! Ernie looks after the very tricky business of balancing and spit-roasting the beast to tender succulence, a task that will take up to 10 hours of his care and attention. The Waldners buy locally raised inspected hogs and prepare them with their own all-natural spice mixtures. Their minimum party is 40 people, but they'd rather have 100.

"A smaller hog doesn't have the high meat-to-bone ratio of the bigger ones," he says wisely. They don't supply any other food, but they'll bring along serving trays, and if you need Ernie to carve, arrange it ahead of time. (Our advice? Don't try this on your own unless you've done it before. Going whole hog sounds easier than it is.)

◉   TABER

Here in the Corn Capital of Canada, their motto is "Come for the corn, stay for the fun." They're talking about the annual two day Cornfest, held every August, with all the corn you'd ever want to eat, and a major food event: a chili and cornbread cookoff.

$ **Pita Pad and Juice Co.**
5335 48th Avenue   (403) 223-7778
Open Monday–Friday 11:00 AM–9:00 PM; Saturday 11:00 AM–7:00 PM
DEBIT

There's good lunch fare here—wraps, pitas, smoothies. They sell Saucy Ladies condiments.

◉   VAUXHALL

"The potato capital of the west" is on Highway 36, and the drive from Taber takes us through irrigated fields of corn and potatoes, and the great rolling country around the Oldman River Dam.

If you're hungry in Vauxhall, there's Wendy's Drive In (not *that* Wendy's) where they fry the chicken from scratch (it's a 20-minute wait) and, in season, they make strawberry milkshakes with ice cream and real strawberries. In the summer, Deacon's Farm Market sets up beside the drive-in with fresh produce.

Sadly, the Rib Cage Grill with its mammoth rib platters has closed and been replaced with the Tan and Tone, which is not a restaurant.

Nona's Pizzeria and Steakhouse

434 2nd Avenue N (403) 654-4223
Open Sunday–Friday 11:00 AM–10:00 PM; Saturday 4:00 PM–10:00 PM
V, MC, AE

Muriel and Tom Belcastro have owned this place for 20 years. If you're hungry for pizza and you're in Vauxhall, this is the spot with over 30 thick crust varieties. They offer three sizes of New York cut steak, and on Sundays they might do a roast beef dinner as a special.

◎ SEVEN PERSONS

Premium Sausage Inc.

Hwy 3, south side (403) 832-2224
Open Monday–Saturday 8:00 AM–6:00 PM
V, MC, DEBIT

We almost rocketed right past Seven Persons, but came to a screeching halt when we spied Ralph Erb's wonderful sausage shop beside the highway. Ralph uses his own recipes for German Mennonite-style sausage, fresh, smoked, dried, frying sausage, garlic coils, smokies, pepperoni, Thuringer, summer sausage, salami, boneless country hams, Black Forest hams, smoked pork chops, shoulder and back bacon—the works. He also sells fresh meat, and his pride and joy is pork jerky, a dark, slightly sweet jerky that's good alone or crumbled into soups or stews for a flavour bonus.

"On a good Saturday we sell $800 worth of pork jerky," says Ralph.

He also handles specialty products from the Dutch Pantry (whoopie pies, saskatoon pies) Lisi's Kitchen (five varieties of kuchen) and Kirschenman Farms, source of Ryan and Kathy's homemade pizza buns, krautbrot, kneppla (noodles), taco pockets (pyrohy filled with ground beef and cheese) and meaty, German-style cabbage rolls.

☺ MEDICINE HAT

Lots of reasons to stop in Medicine Hat—tall trees, the colourful flower baskets along 3rd Street and 4th Street and the friendly atmosphere of a small city. There are a number of notable independent restaurants worth a stop.

We still love the Vineyard (V1 p. 177), with its strong regional menu, VQA wines and its beautiful courtyard awash in flowers during the summer.

After that, there's . . .

$ ### Mad Hatter Roastery

513 3rd Street SE   (403) 529-2344
Open Monday–Friday 7:00 AM–5:30 PM
Saturday 8:00 AM–5:30 PM; Sunday 10:00 AM–5:00 PM
CASH ONLY

> This is a comfortable spot downtown to relax with a cup of good coffee and two of the best in-house desserts we've found—delicious chocolate cake with brown sugar caramel icing and scrumptious carrot cake. They also have good biscotti. Nearly 20 specialty coffees are available, plus the usual variations—espresso, lattes, mochaccino, cappuccino. Owner Kathryn Tatham recently added a line of loose teas.

$ ### City Bakery

317 6th Avenue SE   (403) 527-2800
Open Monday–Saturday 7:00 AM–5:00 PM
Closed every August
V, MC, DEBIT

> We should all be so lucky to have a spot like City Bakery in the neighbourhood. Established in 1960, this busy bakery/café offers fresh bread, coffee and comfort food. A meaty stroganoff with a mellow sour cream sauce, a hearty beef stew with carrots and onions, macaroni and cheese almost the way Mom made it, bagelwiches made with their own bagels. Rye, sourdoughs and country style breads are baked Monday, Wednesday and Friday; white breads Tuesday and Thursday. Sadly, they no longer make dinner buns, but their German-style streusel-topped crumb buns are a local legend. They also sell a variety of cream cheeses for those New York-style bagels. City Bakery packs up its trunk and goes on holiday every August.

Zucchini Blossom Market and Café

$

62 3rd Street NE   (403) 526-1630

Open Monday–Wednesday 8:00 AM–5:00 PM; Thursday, Friday 8:00 AM–9:00 PM
Saturday 9:00 AM–5:00 PM; Sunday 11:00 AM–5:00 PM
V, MC

Yet another Medicine Hat surprise, the Zucchini Blossom is a charming café and gourmet market in a destination block. It sits between The Best Darn Liquor Store Period and a doggie deportment school, just a door away from Café Mauro on the corner.

The curry-coloured room is decorated with giant fiberglass vegetables, the serving dishes are handsome hand-thrown pottery, and the food is simply scrumptious. We sampled a spicy bulgur salad, a couple of outstanding deli-style Italian sandwiches with thin-sliced capicolla and provolone cheese. Also memorable: a fresh green bean salad with a lemon-garlic marinade, tiny shreds of lemon zest, and a touch of grated Parmesan. Also try the pecan-crusted goat cheese served warm on greens with a maple-hazelnut vinaigrette, or the Caprezzi— stacked boconccini, black olive tapenade and fresh heirloom tomatoes on a bed of greens with basil-Dijon vinaigrette. Delicious (!) desserts—lemon slice with fresh-picked raspberries in season, mochaccino cheesecake, crunchy biscotti, and the house-made baklava are especially recommended. Thursday and Friday evenings they offer Mediterranean-style cooking. Be sure to try the Industrial Park Ale, Raspberry Ale, the Velvet Fog and the Brown Ale, all on tap from the Wild Rose Brewing Company in Calgary.

Owners Kristine and Jim Dalzell also stock some good specialty foods. If you're looking for extra-virgin olive or organic canola oil, Gloria vegetable spreads, or delicious full-fat Liberty yogurts, here they are.

3

THE DINOSAUR TRAIL REVISITED

◎ DRUMHELLER

$ **Athens Café**

71 Bridge Street N
(403) 823-9400
Open Monday–Friday 11:00 AM–1:30 PM, 4:00 PM–9:30 PM
Saturday, Sunday 4:00 PM–9:30 PM
V, MC

> The Athens Café, a family-run restaurant just before the bridge, serves an authentic Greek menu, the klefteko, slow-baked lamb with garlic, oregano and other herbs, is one of their best dishes. We also like the kotopoulo, boneless chicken breast, flattened, marinated with lemon and garlic, grilled golden but still juicy. Main courses are served with a good Greek salad (tomatoes, cucumbers, onions, lots of feta cheese) or lemon-roasted potatoes and rice. The pita and spanikopita are homemade. The tzatziki has long, long shreds of cucumber. They do a good steak.
>
> In summer, a lucky duck named Sunshine (the family pet) comes to the restaurant every day, and hangs out in a special pen behind the restaurant, fluffing her snowy feathers, paddling in a brackish wading pool, and generally entertaining anybody who drops by. "No duck on this menu," says Natasha, the duck-friendly waitress.

$ **Whif's Flapjack House**

Badlands Motel
(780) 823-7595
Open daily 6:00 AM–2:00 PM
V, MC, AE, DEBIT

> Owner Lynn Hyatt serves breakfast, brunch or lunch with all the fixin's, and the flapjacks are the genuine article, made from scratch since the day Whif's opened nearly 15 years ago. The eggs are separated, then folded into the beaten whites,

producing a high, tender flapjack that doesn't resemble the dry, powdery, pull-apart-in-the-middle versions that pass in average pancake houses. "That's why we call them flapjacks," says the waitress. Waffles are topped with mixed fresh fruit in season. Also on the menu are filled crepes and loaded omelettes. Service by staff who are proud of the food. Long live Whif's.

Willow Tea Room

East Coulee   (403) 822-3970
Open May long weekend–September long weekend 9:00 AM–5:00 PM
CASH ONLY

Like nearby Wayne, East Coulee was once a lively mining town, and there are people who still remember the typical miner's lunch—a garlic sausage and cheese sandwich. The old brick school in this tiny hamlet has been turned into a museum with a small café (the tea room) in one of the classrooms. Breakfast and lunch are also served here, and although it's not a long menu, it's all home cooking: bacon and eggs for breakfast, the daily soup and a sandwich for lunch, and a roster of homebaked desserts—fruit cobbler or pie. Afternoon tea involves lovely fresh scones, served with strawberry jam. There are a passel of different teas, including chai and Yankee-style iced tea, brewed and chilled without sugar.

FROM VOLUME ONE WE STILL LIKE

We still love the Last Chance Saloon, in Wayne (p. 170), and the Whistling Kettle (p. 170), in Drumheller.

The East Coulee Community Hall Sunday Breakfast

Last Sunday of every month
Open 9:00 AM–1:00 PM

This bountiful brunch is a local fundraiser for the community hall. It's all volunteer labour, local folks helping out. We're talking ham, bacon, sausage, scrambled eggs or fried, toast, pancakes, the works, and the price is about to go up to a whopping $7 per person!

Look for the big pink building. You can't miss it; East Coulee isn't that big.

CALGARY

PANTRY

BAKERIES

Urban Baker

802 Edmonton Trail NE   (403) 266-3763

Open Tuesday–Friday 10:00 AM–9:00 PM

Saturday 9:00 AM–9:00 PM; Sunday 9:00 AM–4:00 PM

V, MC, DEBIT

> Calgary has a lot of really good bread bakeries—Heritage Breadworks, Rustic
> Sourdough, Gunther's, Eiffel Tower for baguette. Now, add the Urban Baker to the
> list. Whitney Armstrong and Dwayne Ennest are partners in this venture, right
> next door to Dwayne's Diner Deluxe. They make exceptional slow-rise, hand-

rolled pain au levain—baguette, apple flax sourdough, country white. They also make foccacia, a sesame black pepper lavash (crispy flatbread) and a decadent yeasted chocolate cranberry loaf ideal for outrageous French toast. The rye flours and all grains are certified organic from Grainworks. The wood-burning oven produces exceptional thin crust pizzas; smoked chicken, Italian sausage with red peppers and a really good Greek pizza with feta, spinach Kalamata olives and oregano.

The bakery is as wonderful on the sweet side, producing homey filling-from-scratch fruit and lemon meringue pies, dreamy crème brulée, ginger cake, squares and an assortment of fine cookies and tarts.

Collective Kitchens Catering
www.cmcn.ab.ca

Talk about "win-win." Through the Collective Kitchens Catering program, the Calgary Mennonite Center for Newcomers is able to provide immigrant women with job experience and a comfortable learning environment, while providing their clients with authentic ethnic food. There are occasionally buffet dinners as well. To order meals, or for more information call Michael Fitzpatrick at (403) 537-8809.

Charlie's Bakery
1247 Kensington Road NW   (403) 670-0850
Open Tuesday–Saturday 10:00 AM–6:00 PM
V, MC, DEBIT

It's becoming a food lover's block: cheese from Janice Beaton, wine from Kensington Wine Market, now bread from Charlie's Bakery—it just opened at deadline. Excellent baguette. Expect the same international flavours and high quality found at sister company Muse Restaurant.

MEAT AND FOWL

Calgary Meats and Deli
1204 Edmonton Trail NE   (403) 276-1423
Open Tuesday–Saturday 8:30 AM–6:00 PM
V, MC, DEBIT

On a bright summer's morning, the proprietor sits outside his spotless shop, visiting with a few customers, smiling at people streaming through the door. They specialize in local and regional meats, Alberta lamb, beef and pork. Their standard for beef is seven-day dry-age, then 21 day in cryovac. Beefophiles can request 21 days of dry-aging. Lots of Valbella products, and the usual European condiments are available.

Horizon Meats

1–3610 29th Street NE (403) 291-0595
Open Tuesday–Friday 9:00 AM–6:00 PM
Saturday 8:00 AM–4:00 PM
V, MC, DEBIT

Certified organic yak meat, anyone? The cheerful butcher shop carries a large range of fresh products—Alberta pork and lamb, all grades of beef and bison. Exotics, too, like ostrich, yak, rattlesnake and alligator on request. They make several fresh and cured sausages including andouille, cheese smokies, and nitrite and gluten free varieties. There's a basic selection of cheeses and some local condiments including Pepperheads (p. 141).

Illichman's Sausage Shop

1840 36th Street SE (403) 272-1673
Open Tuesday–Friday 9:00 AM–6:00 PM
Saturday 8:00 AM–5:00 PM
V, MC, DEBIT

A fixture in the International Avenue area, this old fashioned European style butcher shop produces cold cuts, head cheese, sausage, smokies and bratwurst. There are some prepared foods—potato salad, cabbage rolls, and three tables if you decide to have a sandwich.

Jan's Meat and Delicatessen

2436 2nd Avenue NW (403) 270-8334
Open Tuesday–Saturday 10:00 AM–7:00 PM
DEBIT

Jan's makes their own pickles, big crisp dills right from the barrel. You can buy bread, a selection of cheeses, European condiments, pyrohy and cabbage rolls (with meat). But the real deal is the sausage: lean, garlicky, country-style. We like to pick one up and eat it on the way home.

Mediterranean Meats and Groceries

A3917 17th Avenue SW (403) 272-1119
Open daily 10:00 am–7:00 pm
V, MC, DEBIT

It's a good grocery store for Mediterranean products of all sorts: nuts, olives, oils, syrups, frozen and canned goods. The chewy large Iranian bread sprinkled with za'tar (sumac thyme mix) feeds a crowd. Seasonal produce, look for the cases of succulent figs available in late summer.

Second to None Meats

2100 4th Street SW   (403) 245-6662
Open Tuesday–Thursday, Saturday 9:30 AM–6:00 PM
Friday 9:30 AM–7:00 PM; Sunday 12:00 PM–6:00 PM
V, MC, DEBIT

It's a small, spotless meat market, and Bob and Arlene Choquette are justly proud of their True Taste Piedmontese Beef, Galloway and Highland from the Canadian Celtic Co. Coleen Fowler, who says about their Celtic breeds: "Where was this beef when we first got married? I just can't wreck a roast." They also carry product from Lethbridge's Jam Lady, Canmore's, Valbella Meats, wild salmon; ducks, quail, guinea hens from Quebec.

WHERE GOOD COOKS SHOP

Calgary Farmers' Market Currie Barracks

www.calgarymarket.ca
Hangar #6, 4421 Quesnay Drive SW   (403) 299-4400
Open Friday–Sunday 10:00 AM–3:00 PM

Ron Hamilton of Sunworks Farm was instrumental in forming the Calgary Farmers' Market at Currie Barracks. For several years he and his wife Sheila sold their certified organic pork, chicken and eggs at the Blackfoot Market. A group of interested, likeminded farmers formed a society to refurbish the Currie Barracks and operate the new market.

"Most markets evolve," says Ron. "This market was designed from the ground up by a group of growers."

Currie Barracks opened in spring 2004 and was a hit right off the bat—30,000 people streamed in on opening day, and the numbers haven't let up since. This market is open three days per week, allowing people to use the market as a regular place to shop. "People expect to talk to a farmer," says Ron.

HERE ARE SOME OF OUR FAVOURITE VENDORS:

Innisfail Growers: Four farms make up this co-op: Green Farm, Edgar Farms, The Jungle, and Beck Farms. They grow and sell bedding plants, asparagus, luscious strawberries, summer vegetables, pickles and root vegetables in the fall. You'll find various permutations of these farms at farmers' markets all over the province.

Rustic Sourdough Bakery are known for their hand-formed loaves.

Sylvan Star Cheese from Lacombe (V1 p. 60, 197) sells their wonderful artisan gouda here. Try the award-winning aged cheese.

S.K. Gardens from Vauxhall bring in their beautiful vegetables: sweet Nantes carrots, cucumbers, three different types of field tomatoes which they start from seed, green peppers, eggplants, kohlrabi, lettuces, beets, snow peas, sugar peas. Market day starts early. They are in the fields at 2:30 AM to pick and load the vegetables to get the market for 6:30 AM.

Wapiti Ways, Zona Armstrong's family company, offer 18 products, from frozen elk meat to pillows made from the hides at their stall. One of our favourite chefs, Tim Wood of the Eco Café in Pigeon Lake (V1 p163), uses her elk for the delicious frozen meals on offer in single serving and family size: elk lasagne, prairie gumbo, elk calzone and Asian-style ginger elk.

Hoven Farms near Eckville is known for its certified organic beef. They stock both fresh and frozen meat, and they cut steaks to order. www.hovenfarms.com

Ladybug's Marie Leclerc spent 30 years in the restaurant business in Belgium before coming to Canada for her son's schooling. She's an excellent baker. Try her Belgian waffles, madeleines and palmiers. All are made with high-quality goods—all butter and organic ingredients.

Two Greek Gals is a busy booth with excellent salad and tzatziki for picnic lunches or snacking.

Lorik Farms' Eric and Lorie Ashworth raise free-range pork near Deadwood. We like these guys because they've done the research, know a lot about their animals and pass that information on to their customers. And their pork is excellent—Tamworth and Yorkshire Duroc cross. They believe that pigs raised outdoors have stronger immune systems and are generally healthier.

Valta Bison's Gil and Darlene Hegel raise grain-finished bison on their ranch near Valhalla Centre. Their farm complies with the Canadian Quality Bison Program.

Sunworks Farm raises lamb, chicken and pigs on their farm near Armena. Their stand at Currie Barracks is becoming a mini-grocery store—certified organic milk from Vital Green, near Nobleford, slow rise breads from Infuse Catering of Calgary and Blush Lane Organic (their kids' strawberry and organic produce business). They're also at the Old Strathcona Market in Edmonton (V1 p. 226).

Spaghetti Squash, Farmers' Market Style

Spaghetti squash looks like a yellow football, and when it's cooked, the inside flesh shreds into delicate fibres—thus the name "spaghetti squash." They're grown all over Alberta and are easy to find in farmers' markets during harvest season. Spaghetti squash has become one of the favourite vegetables at the Upper Crust, an Edmonton restaurant.

To cook: Bring a large pot of water to a boil. Ease in your squash, and cook until the skin can be easily pierced with a fork. Let it cool. Halve, and scoop out the seeds and excess stringy bits. Using a fork, shred the flesh, end to end. It will look like spaghetti. Toss the hot strands with a little melted butter, salt, pepper and 1 cup (or more) of shredded cheese. We like Leoni Grana Parmesan, or an aged gouda from Sylvan Star.

Roasted Green Tomato Soup
La P'tite Table

Chef Thierry Meret of La P'tit Table, a delightful French country restaurant in the heart of Okotoks (V1 p. 6), makes this delicious soup in the fall, with the last of the field tomatoes. We also tried this soup substituting garlic sausage and found it delicious.

3.5 lbs (1.5 k) firm green tomatoes, cored, halved
2 tbsp (30 mL) vegetable oil
2 medium onions, sliced thin
6 garlic cloves, sliced
3 celery stalks, sliced
6 Alberta lamb Merguese sausage
2 bay leaves
10 cups (2.5 L) chicken stock
2 large Bintge or Yukon Gold potatoes, peeled, diced
handful chopped fresh cilantro
½ cup (125 mL) white wine
¼ tsp (2 mL) Tabasco sauce
2 tsp (10 mL) natural hickory liquid smoke
1 tsp (5 mL) sugar
salt to taste

To finish:
½ cup (125 mL) whipping cream, room temperature
2 tbsp (30 mL) butter

Grill tomatoes on a hot barbecue, turning several times. Cool and dice. Cook onions in oil until soft but not coloured. Add garlic, celery, sausages, bay leaves. Cook 5 minutes. Remove sausages, cool, slice and reserve. Add tomatoes and cilantro and cook another 10 minutes. Add chicken stock and diced potato. Bring to a boil. Add remaining ingredients and turn down the heat. Cover and simmer about 45 minutes, until potatoes fall apart. Let soup cool. Purée in a blender, working in small batches. Strain through a sieve and correct the seasoning.

To serve: reheat soup. Whisk in whipping cream and butter. Ladle into bowls and top with sliced sausages.

Option: A spoonful of curry-spiked sour cream may be added over the sausages.
Serves 8 to 10

Crossroads Market

1235 26th Avenue SE, corner of Ogden Road & Blackfoot Trail   (403) 291-5208

Open Friday–Sunday 9:00 AM–5:00 PM

A large indoor flea market-style market with some good food. We like Kaman Pies, especially the buffalo shepherds pie. Chongo's Market is a busy indoor/outdoor fruit stand with excellent variety in Okanagan fruit in season (14 different varieties of cherries) and good imported tropical specialties.

Fiasco Gelato

736 17th Avenue SW (Main location)   (403) 229-2503

Sunday–Wednesday 9:00 AM–11:00 PM

Thursday–Saturday 9:00 AM–12:00 AM

V, MC, DEBIT

Matt Wilson makes ice cream like an Italian. His 24 flavours of gelato (tartufo, espresso, kiwi) are made with milk. The sorbetto (lemon, local blackcurrant) are made with fresh ingredients and no milk, as it should be. He makes several kinds for local restaurants, including a unique parmesan gelato for Quarry in Canmore. You can have it by the cup, or take home a half or full litre. Panini and Illy Caffe are also on offer at his cheery shop with the tomato red coolers and lime-coloured walls. There are two other locations: 207 10 Street NW and 807 1 Street SW.

Haute and Humble to go   www. hautehumble.com

1516 6th Street SW   (403) 802-0044

Open Monday–Saturday 10:00 AM–7:00 PM

Sundays 12:00 AM–5:00 PM

V, MC, DEBIT

A small storefront just off busy 17th Avenue with well-made takeaway items. Boxed hot lunches, personal chef services, catering. Eclectic menu: soups, pasta, meat pies, unusual vegetable sides, terrific salads. Think of triple cheese and wild mushroom lasagne; braised lamb shanks meat pie; lots of comforting, healthy-type items to go, plus some groovy high-end condiments—truffle oils, Palette Fine Foods items, good olive oils, plus specialty breads from Vancouver's Ecco e Pane Bakery.

Janice Beaton Fine Cheese

www.jbfinecheese.com

1249 Kensington Road NW   (403) 283-0999

Open Tuesday–Friday 9:00 AM–7:00 PM

Saturday 9:00 AM–6:00 PM; Sunday 11:00 AM–5:00 PM

V, MC, DEBIT

Janice Beaton has opened a second cheese shop (the first is described in V1 p. 13). Handily, it's just down the street from Kensington Wine Market. Expect the same wonderful selection of cheeses, plus the added self-service area with a larger selection of Hotchkiss produce. It's next door to Muse Bakery, so you can pick up bread along with the cheese.

Mercato

2224 4th Street SW   (403) 263-5535

Open Monday–Saturday 11:00 AM–6:00 PM

V, MC, AE, DEBIT

An Italophile's heaven. Bridgeland's loss is 4th Street's gain. What we loved in Bridgeland—the Italian Center, the Italian Gourmet Foods pasta, the Scuola Cucina cooking school, and the excellent Merlo Vinoteca wine store, have now moved under one roof in a former Tony Roma's. Co-founder Victor Caracciolo's son Domenic is the guy responsible. Lovely displays; platters of heirloom tomatoes. Domenic has plans for a cappuccino bar, wine bar and expanded tastings. More cooking classes too, we hope.

Phillips Forbidden Flavours

101–1013 17th Avenue SW   (403) 244-2697

783 Northmount Road NW   (403) 282-8666

Open Monday–Friday 12:00 PM–9:00 PM

Saturday, Sunday and holidays 1:00 PM–9:00 PM

V, MC, DEBIT

Here are some of the most exotic ice cream flavours we've tasted—black sesame seed, green tea, durian, purple taro, wasabi. He makes a lovely coconut ice cream, as well as kid-friendly flavours. How about worms in dirt? (That would be chocolate cookies 'n cream with gummy bears.)

Red Tree Kitchen www.redtreecatering.com
2129 33rd Avenue SW (403) 242-3246
Open Monday–Friday 10:00 AM–7:00 PM
Saturday 10:00 AM–6:00 PM
V, MC, DEBIT

Aaron Creurer and Susan Hopkins have opened this attractive provisioning spot in Marda Loop. It's a beautiful space with baby gold walls and aged terracotta floor, attached to their catering kitchen and production space. You can have fresh meals for one, frozen for two—butter chicken, Galloway beef, dips, spreads, crudites, Eiffel Tower breads. You'll also find exceptional home-style baking: squares, biscotti, cookies, and the ineffable chocolate Diablo cake.

WINE SHOPS

Bin 905 www.bin905.com
2311 4th Street SW (403) 261-1600
Open Monday–Saturday 10:00 AM–8:00 PM; Sunday 12:00 PM–6:00 PM
V, MC, AE, DEBIT

A fabulous selection for the oenophile: Jermann, Krug, Staglin Family, Jacques Prieur. It's not all big ticket though—there's lots of value in them thar hills, though you may have to redefine your definition of value. The shop is owned by the Canadian Rocky Mountain Resorts people and well managed by Geoff Last who writes a wine column for the *Calgary Herald*. The newly built tasting room will handle the burgeoning requests for classes and tastings.

The Cellar www.cellarwinestore.com
100–137 8th Avenue SW (403) 503-0730
Open Monday–Wednesday 10:30 AM–6:00 PM
Thursday, Friday 10:00 AM–8:00 PM
Saturday 10:00 AM–6:00 PM; Sunday 12:00 PM–6:00 PM

A comprehensive selection from all wine regions. Excellent Canadian choices with some scarce bottlings from Naramata Bench and Oliver areas. It's a gorgeous space in the basement of the historic Alberta Hotel building, right around the corner from Murrieta's. Their newsletter is informative and timely. The enthusiastic staff offers tastings, classes, wine gadgets and accoutrements in a browser-friendly environment. Sandrina Kiltzof Blue Grouse Vineyard on Vancouver Island is part of this team.

The Wine Cellar

600–9737 Macleod Trail S　　　　　　　　　　　　　　(403) 640-1111

Open Monday–Friday 10:00 AM–9:30 PM

Saturday 10:00 AM–8:00 PM; Sunday 11:00 AM–6:30 PM

V, MC, AE, DEBIT

Frank Kennedy took the store over from Calgary wine pioneer Joeseph de'Angelis. It's now affiliated with the Wine Cellar in Edmonton. Strengths are in France, Australia and California bottlings with several exclusive labels—Two Hands from the Barossa Valley; Poetry from Cliff Lede Vineyards in California. This is an easy place to shop—nice people who know their stuff and help you out to the car with your goodies. Their long-running Cellar Builder program is an excellent way to do just that: build a collection of keeping-quality wines with minimal time and effort.

COOKS' TOOLS

The Art of Hardware

1001 10th Avenue SW　　　　　　　　　　　　　　(403) 244-4960

Monday–Friday 8:00–6:00 PM; Saturday 10:00 AM–6:00 PM

V, MC, AE, DEBIT

This is all about luxe hardware for kitchen and home. Owner Jeanne Milne used to renovate houses and she fell in love with all the neat stuff for kitchens, things she would see in magazines but couldn't find here. The store is filled with both the practical and the whimsical. Renovating the kitchen? Check out the oh-so-groovy pot filler faucets: the Melrose and the Creation in either chrome or satin nickel. Edmonton kitchen freaks, be patient. The Art of Hardware plans a location on 124th Street.

Jolle Chef

6457 42nd Avenue SE　　　　　　　　　　　　　　(403) 256-5555

Monday–Friday 9:00 AM–5:00 PM; Saturday 10:00 AM–5:00 PM

V, MC, AE, DEBIT

Former chef Michael Marks and wife Mickey own this large kitchen supply house. They started with a mobile knife sharpening service and the business grew from there. All the big names in knives are stocked: Wusthof–Trident, Global, Henkel, Sabatier, Swibo, Kyocera. Cookware lines include Cuisinart, All-Clad and Lacor. All the Riedel crystal is carried: Overture, Restaurant Series, Vinum, Vinum Extreme, Sommelier, plus the trendy, stemless O Series. ("Can't keep it in stock," says Michael.) They carry every kitchen gadget known to man (or woman): Silicon brushes, spatula, molds, silpat mats, strainers, food mills and so on. It's an experience not to be missed.

CALGARY EVENTS

Wine Stage, Calgary's Most Dramatic Wine Event, is a fundraiser for One Yellow Rabbit Performance Theatre. Past events have poured wines from Bin 905, Metrovino, J. Webb Wine Merchant, Kensington, The Banff Wine Store with dishes from Divino, The Living Room, Sugo and River Café among others. Call (403) 264-3224 for information or tickets.

Slow Food Stampede Garden Party at Rouge is a walkabout meal in their large garden with local producers. Top Calgary chefs do the cooking. Slow Food Feast of Fields celebrates the harvest by pairing Calgary chefs with local farmers and producers. Tickets for slow food events are available at Janice Beaton Fine Cheese and the Cookbook Co. Cooks. www.slowfoodcalgary.com

Around the World in 35 Blocks is International Avenue's long running tour of the sweet and savoury ethnic shops and purveyors in the Forest Lawn area of 17th Avenue SE. If you love food, this is the tour, with East Indian, Middle Eastern, Latin American and European foods all available. Lots of sampling. These bus tours sell out fast. (403) 248-7288; www.internationalavenue.ca.

Dine Alberta is the annual autumn program highlighting local ingredients and regional producers in over 70 restaurants throughout the province. Watch for it in September each year. www.dinealberta.ca.

The California Wine Fair comes to town in late February, launching two weeks of wine, the arts and downtown dining events. www.savourcalgary.com.

Barbecue on the Bow
Labour Day Weekend

www.bbqonthebow.com

Now in its 13th year, this meaty event started as the Alberta Barbecue Championship in Eau Claire market. It's a slow smokin', pork pullin' kinda party, sanctioned by the Kansas City Barbecue Society for southern style barbecue. Each team must smoke four food groups—pork butt, pork ribs, beef brisket, and a chicken, slowly, over coals and wood. Local barbecue stars are Kathy (Queen Butt Shredder) Richardier of the award winning Rockin' Ronnies', and Dave (King Brisket Boy) Thurgar. It's a free, fun, family event held in the heart of Calgary's downtown Eau Claire Market. There's a public barbecue pit serving pulled pork and brisket, cooking demos, and other activities for the whole family.

Road food

Blackfoot Truck Stop (Petrocan)   (403) 265-5964
1840 9th Avenue SE
Open 24 hours
V, MC AMEX, DEBIT

Get your road food here. This busy truck stop smells good, like somebody's kitchen after a weekend fry-up, rather than the usual old grease and stale cigarette smoke. The food's not remarkable—frozen fries, sandwiches on thin white sandwich bread— but it's an appealing joint all the same. The breakfast special was home fries with sausages, eggs and coffee. The veggie omelette was excellent. We like the old-fashioned side menu: sliced bananas with milk, canned pears or peaches on toast. Don't bother with the beans—they're canned too. It's a big room with lots of trucker memorabilia and a segregated smoking room.

The Oyster King

Neptune Oyster Company   (403) 244-1621

Tony Wing came west to develop the oyster program at Catch. He's deep into oyster culture. He's worked with Michael Stadlander and has participated internationally at oyster shucking competitions. He has suffered for his craft, blowing out his elbow at a recent competition. ("It's the same movement tennis players use," he says.)

Neptune Oyster Co. supplies oysters to Calgary restaurants. He'll advise on set up, bring in the best oysters from both coasts and develop staff into champion shuckers. He is also for hire—if you want an oyster bar at your next party Tony's your man. He can shuck with the best of them; came fourth in the Canadian Nationals (in Oyster Shucking) last year. Six oysters in 20 seconds is his pace.

Tony is also known around town as the calendar guy. He's responsible for the Chef's of Calgary Calendar fundraiser for Collective Kitchens. Look for your favourite chefs—handsome Cam Dobranski of Muse is Mr. June.

Aida's Lebanese Food

2208 4th Street SW   (403) 541-1189

Open Monday 11:00 AM–9:00 PM; Tuesday–Thursday 11:00 AM–10:00 PM

Friday, Saturday 11:00 AM–11:00 PM

V, MC, AE, DEBIT

> This casual restaurant is dead serious about good food. Start with the mouham-
> mara made with roasted peppers, onion, finely ground walnuts and pomegranate
> juice served with warm pita. Move on to the spicy halibut or the unusual and
> tasty fish tagine with tahini and pine nuts. The lamb chops in a secret herb mari-
> nade are memorable, as is the fatouche salad, one of those simple dishes that acts
> as the canary in the coal mine: good fatouche is a signal that all is right in the
> kitchen.

Anpurna

175B 52nd Street SE   (403) 235-6028

Open Tuesday–Friday 11:00 AM–2:30 PM; 5:00 AM–8:30 PM

Saturday, Sunday 11:00 AM–8:30 PM

V, DEBIT

> This simple, family-run spot serves outstanding vegetarian food from Gujarati
> province in western India. We love the masala dossa: spiced potatoes with onions
> in a crepe with lentil dahl. The chutneys are delicious—little flavour explosions
> of coriander or coconut. Combination plates (called thali) have vegetable curries
> and assorted sides of dhal, rice, roti and Indian pickle.

Avenue Diner

103 8th Avenue SW   (403) 263-2673

Open Monday–Friday 7:00 AM–3:00 PM; Saturday, Sunday 8:00 AM–3:00 PM

V, MC, AE, ENR, DEBIT

> The Avenue is our favourite place to start the day downtown—grilled grapefruit
> with house-made rosemary syrup, and incredible barley porridge. They're
> famous for their mac 'n' cheese made with applewood smoked cheddar cheese
> and a little chardonnay. You can tart it up by adding truffled portabella mush-
> rooms, capicolla, or smoked salmon and chives. The luscious local beef burger
> comes with truffled portabella and provolone. Fixin's for the eggs benny change
> with the seasons.
>
> They use a lot of seasonal regional ingredients—buffalo short ribs, braised

overnight 'til fork tender, served with native black cherries, and Sturgeon Valley pork chop with sweet potato and warm apple marmalade. Watch for the cheerful scarlet tractor seats along the counter. Heather rescued them from a farm in central Alberta, then had them painted at a body shop.

Crete Souvlaki

$

2623 17th Avenue SW   (403) 246-4777

Open daily 7:00 AM–10:30 PM

V, MC, DEBIT

A chef told us about this spot. Otherwise we'd have missed it entirely, tucked as it is into a gas station-cum-convenience store. (A bit dodgy, that.) But the food changes everything. Cheap and cheerful, with the best lamb souvlaki and tzatziki this side of Heraklion.

Café de Tokyo

$

630 1st Avenue NE   (403) 264-20276

Open Monday 5:00 PM–9:00 PM

Tuesday–Friday 11:30 AM–2:00 PM, 5:00 PM–9:00 PM; Saturday 12:00 PM–9:00 PM

CASH ONLY

This modest restaurant tucked away in a strip mall close to Bridgeland is a local favourite. Peaceful and homey, it has six tables and four stools at the sushi bar. Pristine sushi, made by deft hands. The gyoza (small fried dumplings) are light and flavourful, never greasy. The miso ramen (noodle soup with fermented soybean paste) is restorative.

Clay Oven

$$

349–3132 26th Street NE   (403) 250-2161

Open Monday–Saturday 11:30 AM–2:00 PM, 5:00 AM–9:00 PM

V, MC, AE, ENR, DEBIT

We don't know how we missed this outstanding family-run restaurant in the first Food Lover's Trail Guide, big fans of Indian food that we are. The chicken tikka is particularly good, as is the rich malaikofta (paneer in tomato cream). Don't leave without trying the eggplant bharta. The eggplant is grilled, skin on, to get nice and smoky, then mixed with tomato, chilies, onions, and spiced with their own masala, cumin seed, ginger and garlic. It gives you an excuse to have more of their amazing naan. There is a good lunch buffet (not an oxymoron here).

Gruman's Deli   www.grumansdeli.com

Plaza 1000, 7th Avenue SW (Nova Chemical Building)   (403) 261-9003

Open Monday–Friday 7:30 AM–5:00 PM

Saturday 10:00 AM–4:00 PM

V, MC, AE, ENR. DEBIT

Imagine a Montreal deli with a sit-down restaurant, full meals and takeaway, in a terrific space, operated by a really good chef. That's pretty much what you've got in Gruman's. Peter Fraiberg, one of the original Savoir Fare trio, puts together fine dining and foods from a childhood in Montreal: whole brisket, house-made sauerkraut, chicken matso ball soup and smoked meat sandwiches. His mom came in to teach the bakers how to make the rugelach and traditional mandel-bread. There are more contemporary dishes as well, with a full line-up of good breakfast items: eggs benny, challah, French toast, great sandwiches—think of chicken club with pancetta. Lots of familiar faces from Savoir Fare; chef Paul Orr and Linda Nainaar in the front of the house. The space can be booked for cater-ing and special events in the evenings.

Mango Shiva

507 8th Avenue SW   (403) 290-1644

Monday–Saturday 11:30 AM–2:00 PM; 5:00 PM–9:00 PM

Sunday 5:00 AM–9:00 PM

V, MC, DEBIT

Here's an inspired new-wave South Asian menu, with some classical influence. Think of honey-basil crab samosa, or steamed curried mussels with garlic naan. Then try the tandoori-style wild salmon, or trout in banana leaf. We love the slow-roasted Indian eggplant with a spicy cilantro sauce, yellow lentils and minted peas.

For dessert a chai-tea custard with tamarind-cashew sables, or gulab-jaman with mango sorbet and coconut foam. There's a more traditional buffet at lunch. The lassis (yogurt drinks) are delightful and unusual, a subtle rosewater version, or salted, with cumin, also delicious. Chef Nathan Wright says owner Kam Dhillon hired him to "make the food look as good as it tasted. No more rice and curry plopped on the plate, " he says.

Sugo Café Italia

1214 9th Avenue SE   (403) 263-1115 R

Open daily 5:00 PM–10:00 PM

V, MC, AE, DEBIT

Angelo Contrada and Jessie Trento have expanded their Inglewood restaurant, Sugo, to 50 seats by taking over the shop next door, but it's still an intimate,

relaxed place to enjoy their daily menu of fresh market cuisine. The style is contemporary Italian, using fresh, seasonal and regional ingredients. At deadline there was talk of opening for lunch. It's a well-chosen wine list with several by the glass—whatever Angelo and Jessie think works with the dishes on offer that night. We're glad there's a Sugo.

$$ **Village Cantina**   www.villagecantina.ca
1413 9th Avenue SE   (403) 265-5739
Open Tuesday–Thursday 11:00 AM–11:00 PM
Saturday 9:00 AM–4:00 PM, 7:00 PM–12:00 AM; Sunday 9:00 AM–3:00 PM
V, MC, DEBIT

Owner Linda Crossley started off with pie and coffee, but that soon morphed into a casual restaurant filled with tchotchkes and offering live entertainment. (The long-running Carly's Angels is a kick on Saturday nights.) It's a great neighbourhood joint; even the two resident birds, Dick and Bert, say hello. Weekend breakfast is excellent, especially the frittatas and eggs benny. They take good tequila seriously here, offering flights of 100 per cent blue agave tequilas to sample and compare. Leave room for pie—it's still some of the best in town.

$ **Peter's Drive Inn**
212 16A Avenue NW   (403) 277-2747
Open 9:00 AM–12:00 PM
CASH ONLY

Gus Peter's drive-in is a Calgary institution, having served thousands of burgers for over 40 years. Burgers are heavily sauced, sometimes downright sloppy—if you want it dry, say so. We love the banana milkshake, one of 24 flavours.

Gus is especially proud of the buns, made from a secret recipe by Westin Bakery. "Happy staff is the key to business," says Gus, and some of them have been happy there for more than thirty years.

Simone's

636 10th Avenue SW   (403) 263-6661 R
Open Monday 11:00 AM–2:00 PM
Tuesday–Friday 11:00 AM–2:00 PM, 5:00 PM–close; Saturday 5:00 PM–close
V, MC, AE

> Impeccably fresh spinach salad with warm rolls for starters, then excellent duck—crispy skin, juicy flesh, subtle undertone of fresh orange. The sticky pudding is worth the calories—light, warm with a splash of bourbon and lots of good vanilla. We like this handsome room with cream-coloured leather furniture and interesting art. There's a pleasant bar within the dining room. Short but well-chosen wine list.

Istanbul Restaurant

4–1420 9th Avenue SE   (403) 229-0542
Open Monday–Saturday 11:30 AM–10:30 PM
Sunday 12:00 AM–10:00 PM
V, MC. AE, DEBIT

> It's a family deal, with father Necmettin Ozkan, son Yasin Ozkan, and chef Mahmut Elbasi all involved. This small, sweetly old-fashioned room with its Turkish home cooking would be right at home off an Istanbul market street. We've tried most of this menu, including the slipper-shaped pizza-like turnover (kir pidesi), which comes with fresh parsley and feta filling, or six others, available only during the week. For a bit of everything, there's the Turkish feast for two or more: the sultan's feast involves kisir (bulgur wheat salad loaded with fresh parsley and lemon, similar to tabouleh), deliciously creamy humus, stuffed vine leaves, meat-stuffed zucchini and lamb shish kebab. Whole lamb is available for catered parties; belly dancing on weekends.

Los Mariachas

1–7400 Macleod Trail SE   (403) 253-5692
Open Sunday–Wednesday 11:00 AM–9:00 PM; Thursday–Saturday 11:00 AM–10:00 PM
V, MC, DEBIT

> Two small rooms, cheerful, comfortable, in an unremarkable storefront on busy Macleod Trail with some seriously tasty Mexican food. They have all the standard dishes, including fresh guacamole with chips, chimichangas, that sort of thing. Among the soups is the sopa Azteca, chicken broth with avocado, cheese, peppers and tortilla strips. Well-made chicken enchiladas had three distinctly different fresh sauces: cilantro-laced tomatillo, tomato and a good mole, neither too chocolatey nor too bitter. Or you could try the chicken mole, pork chops in

adobe sauce, camarones (jumbo shrimp) with spicy red creole sauce, and red snapper Veracruz.

$$ **The Siding Café**

100 7th Avenue SW (Arts Central)   (403) 262-0282

Open Sunday 8:00 AM–6:00 PM; Monday–Wednesday 7:00 AM–7: 00 PM

Thursday–Friday 7:00 AM–9:00 PM

Saturday 8:00 AM–9:00 PM

V, MC, AE, DEBIT

> The diner food is fun, and we love the crisp, skinny, house-cut fries and well-made burgers, the torn chicken salad with artichoke hearts, kalamata olives, cherry tomatoes. Some different touches: How about frank-and-beans: stewed white beans with braised elk, whiskey-buffalo sausage. The waiter rushes over with a treat for afters, a demi-tasse with Jones orange pop over vanilla sorbet— just like a liquid creamsicle. It's a designer diner, part of the Murietta's organization, complete with communal table, lots of mirrors and shiny chrome, and stylish red-and-black colour scheme. Upstairs is the Palette Coffeehouse, a coffee-and-pastry spot run by the same folks.

$$ **Boccavino Lounge and Grill**

2220 Centre Street NE   (403) 276-2030

Sunday–Wednesday 11:00 AM–11:00 PM

Thursday–Saturday 11:00 AM–2:00 AM

V, MC, DEBIT

> Tom and Lina Castle (of Lina's fame) opened this trattoria/bar featuring casual Italian food early in 2005. Recommended are the lamb skewers rosticini, grilled with rosemary in their state-of-the-art Woodstone oven. The high dry heat in this oven also produces a terrific thin-crust pizza. Try the rich, traditional lasagne, or their calamari, breaded, with a light herb-tomato sauce. Lina has assembled an enviable team, with chef Sabrino Talbi, and Adamo Eremita in front-of-house.

$$ **Big T's Cookhouse and Smokeshack**

2138 Crowchild Trail NW   (403) 284-5959

8330 Macleod Trail S   (403) 252-5550

Open Daily 11:00 AM–11:00 PM

V, MC, AE, DEBIT

> Southern-style barbecue is what they do, with a third location about to open in the former Arden Diner space on 17th Avenue. Deep-fried dill pickle? Believe it.

Two sharing platters, just right for the some-of-everything crowd: Big T, and the Elvis. (Alas, no deep-fried peanut butter and banana sandwich.) Big T's platter includes substantial portions of sliced beef brisket, pulled pork, smoked St. Louis ribs, dusty rib end (smoked dry rib), Spolumbo's andouille sausage, corn, creamy coleslaw and baked beans with a touch of molasses and apple juice.

Make room for the pecan pie with a splash of Wild Turkey.

BIG NIGHTS, SPLURGES & CELEBRATIONS

$$ **Da Paolo Ristorante**

121 17th Avenue SW   (403) 228-5556 R

Open Monday–Friday 11:30 AM–2:00 PM, 5:00 PM–11:00 PM

Saturday 5:00 PM–11:00 PM

V, MC, AE

The modest exterior of Claudio Carnali and Paulo De Minico's long-time Calgary restaurant belies the elegant interior in calm, soothing colours. This is exquisite Northern Italian food, the cooking subtle and accomplished. Bountiful antipasti and house-made pasta including canneloni with rabbit and porcini stuffed ravioli. The service is finely tuned and never stuffy, with the assurance borne of experience that allows the host to relax, knowing everything will unfold exactly as it should.

$$ **Divino**   www.divinobistro.com

113 8th Avenue SW   (403) 410-5555 R

Open Monday–Friday 11:00 AM–2:00 PM, 5:00 PM–10:00 PM

Saturday, Sunday 5:00 AM–10:00 PM

V, MC, AE

The new Divino is gorgeous—exposed brick walls, rich colours, upscale table accoutrements. It's more downtown chic than the previous version, yet no less charming. They call it American bistro cooking (as opposed to French bistro, we guess). Meats are prepared in the wood-burning grill brought from the Gramercy Tavern in New York. There's a wood-burning pizza oven for flatbreads. All this wood burning does lend a distinct woodsy tang to the air, quickening the appetite. The marble counter holds an extraordinary selection of international cheeses at perfect ripeness and serving temperature. Excellent wine list by sommelier Brad Royale, with superb Italian and American selections. The list won the gold medal at the 2004 Vancouver Wine Festival.

Muse Restaurant and Lounge

107 10A Street NW   (403) 670-6873 R

Open 5:00 PM—10:00 PM

V, MC, AE, DEBIT

> Edmonton chef Cam Dobranski has taken over from David Cox, and his whimsical, inventive cooking style suits the theatrical interior of this restaurant. The lobster lasagne is still their signature dish: Yukon gold potatoes with cream cheese, poached lobster and scallops in a red sauce. Think of green-tea marinated duck breast with zucchini rosti, or veal striploin with sweet potato, pistachio and prosciutto in a veal reduction with melted spinach. For dessert, there's a chocolate tasting. Once we had a tiny carrot cake with carrot chips and a sweet carrot sorbet. The chef makes almost everything in house, including his own pasta and ice creams. Features change constantly.

PHOTO COURTESY CAM DOBRANSKI

Piato Greek House

www.piatogreekhouse.com

1114 Edmonton Trail NE   (403) 277-3408 R

Open daily 5:00 PM—10:00 PM

V, MC, DEBIT

> Chef/owner Dwayne Ennest explores foods of the Mediterranean, emphasizing Greek traditions, ingredients and cooking styles in a contemporary fashion. It's not your standard taverna or souvlaki house. Rather, it's a lovely dining room in which to enjoy great flavours, paired with a unique wine list containing several new to the market, "try-worthy" Greek wines. Start with a selection of meze,

then the scallop tabouli—two barely cooked bay scallops with a foie gras aioli. Savoy cabbage leaves are stuffed with lamb and bulgur and served on creamy, garlicky tzatziki. The signature lamb is a six-chop rack, marked on the grill, finished in the oven, served with figs and a balsamic honey reduction. It's sublime.

Rouge

$$

www.rougerestaurant.com
1240 8th Avenue SE (403) 531-2767 R
Open Monday–Friday 11:30 AM–2:00 PM, 5:30 PM–10:00 PM
Saturday 5:30 PM–10:00 PM
V, MC, AE, DEBIT

Paul Rogalski and Olivier Reynaud have created a gem of a restaurant in the old Cross house, now an official historic site.

The stately Victorian mansion is surrounded by productive working gardens where they grow their own tomatoes, lettuces, herbs and berries. The food is seasonal and changes constantly, ranging from cigar-smoked duck breast, rack of lamb from Dryview Farms with leek risotto. Desserts? Crabapple crème brulée from their own fruit. There's also an astonishingly good wine list.

The Sultan's Tent

$$

909 17th Avenue SW (403) 244-2333 R
Open Monday–Thursday 5:30–10:30 PM; Friday–Saturday 5:00 AM–11:00 AM
V, MC, AE, ENR, DEBIT

The six-course Sultan's feast begins with the North African lentil soup called harira, and four traditional marinated salads—broiled green pepper with fresh tomato; carrot with cinnamon; potato with onion; beet with orange blossom water, onion and parsley. Choose an entrée from the large selection of tagines (chicken, lamb, rabbit, prawn) or the couscous, served with the requisite seven vegetables. To finish, there's dessert (braewat, a very sweet pastry similar to baklava, but with almonds baked into it) and the elaborate mint tea ceremony, with tea poured from a great height.

Low brass tables, couches and comfy cushions and subtle lighting make this a sexy, entertaining way to eat dinner.

Auburn Saloon

115 9th Avenue SE   (403) 266-6628

Open Monday–Friday 11:00 AM–2:00 PM

Saturday, Sunday 5:00 PM–2:00 AM

> This is still a great after-work bar. The chef, Arlene Zevnik, makes a mean meat-loaf sandwich. It's a Big Rock bar with Grasshoppper, Warthog and Honey Brown on tap.

Mynt Ultralounge

www.mynt.ca

516c 9th Avenue SW   (403) 229-9029

Open 4:00 PM–2:00 AM

V, MC, DEBIT

> The place to see and be seen, dance and flirt among cabana-style booths and wandering musicians. There's a huge dance floor and three accommodating bars, including the O Room, complete with its own DJ spinning funky house, which can be booked for exclusive parties and VIP nights. Upstairs (street level) musicians take turns performing in spectacular glass cages suspended over the stairs, then roam about, creating the back beat to the sensual vocal house music. During the summer, the sunken roof top patio, surrounded by warm brick and the skyline is a great spot to start or end an evening. Good sushi and a small tapas menu prepared by Muse.

FROM VOLUME ONE WE STILL LIKE

Diner Deluxe (403) 276-5499 (p. 40); River Café (403) 261-7670 (p. 53); Teatro (403) 290-1012 (p. 53); Living Room (403) 228-9830 (p. 42); La Chaumière (403) 228-5690 (p. 52); Il Sogno (403) 232-8901 (p. 51); Brava Bistro (403) 228-1854 (p. 37); The Ranche (403) 225-3939 (p. 52); Cilantro (403) 229-1177 (p. 50)

⊚ CANMORE

Once a small town on the way to Banff, Canmore is now a destination. The pretty town-site, dominated by the shadow of the Three Sisters, offers world-class skiing on its doorstep and some of the most expensive real estate in the province. Good restaurants are part of the scene here, with several chefs making serious efforts to work with local producers and serve regional specialties.

PANTRY
BAKERIES

JK Bakery
1514 Railway Avenue   (403) 678-4232
Monday–Saturday 7:30 AM–5:00 PM
V, MC, DEBIT

Artisan baker John Kirchpfennig makes his bread the old-fashioned way. The donut-shaped Mediterranean bread and loaves of ciabatta have the chewy crust and big eyes that come from a slow, cold rise and no fat in the dough. Other breads to savour: whole wheat; dark Russian, medium German or seeded Norwegian rye; the flax bread; the multi-grain; the dense, slightly sweet fruit loaf; the cinnamon loaf, excellent toasted with butter. They also make a yeast-free, wheat-free spelt bread. The coffee shop serves soups, pies, pastries and sandwiches.

Sweet Madeira
109–110 Kananaskis Way   (780) 609-9957
Open most afternoons

Cecilia Lortscher and her husband operated a catering business for several years in Canmore while she wrote about life and food for the *Canmore Leader*, eventually publishing a book of columns. After a divorce, Cecilia decided to make baking a full-time occupation.

She is a gifted baker. The cookies are exquisite, heavenly mouthfuls of flavour. Her top ten include the peanut butter lifeworks cookie—a mountain-healthy jumble of oatmeal, raisins and peanut butter; gingersnaps; chocolate shortbread; and a delicious cranberry pistachio that developed out of a desire to use leftover egg yolks. Cecilia makes a lovely currant cake and a rich, buttery Madeira cake, featured by at least one local bed and breakfast. She also makes cinnamon rolls and homestyle brownies, cakes and pies. Her jumbleberry and apple pies are also available at the Flatbread Company. She has developed a mini-biscotti called chompsticks in clever Chinese takeout packaging.

Her cookies can be purchased at the intimate 500-square-foot shop and at both Nosh Food Market and the Flatbread Company.

WHERE GOOD COOKS SHOP

Lavender Harvest Farms

108–737 7th Avenue

Monday–Wednesday 10:00 AM–6:00 PM

Thursday–Saturday 9:30 AM–8:00 PM; Sunday 10:00 AM–5:30 PM

www.lavenderharvestfarms.com

(403) 678-1883

Bow Valley residents Rose and Neil Tanner grow lavender on their farm near Oliver BC and sell it through this lovely shop just off Main Street. You'll find foodstuffs made from lavender and honey, subtle almond orange biscotti made by our favourite cookie lady in Canmore, Sweet Madeira, and lavender-scented chocolates. Company's Coming worked with Lavender Harvest farms to develop a cookbook using lavender and herbes des provence. The cookbook is sold at the store with sachets of culinary lavender. As well, the shop has an attractive selection of tabletop and kitchen accessories.

"Anything we could possibly find with a sprig a lavender on it," says shop assistant Helen McAleenan.

Nosh Food Market

102–817 Main Street

Monday–Friday 10:00 AM–6:00 PM

Saturday 9:00 AM–5:00 PM; Sunday 10:00 AM–5:00 PM

V, MC, DEBIT

(780) 609-6631

Heather and Randy Barker opened Nosh in April 2004. "We had weekended in Canmore for years. When we moved here we missed some of the specialty products we were used to buying in Calgary," said Heather. Things like Mercato fresh pasta, Fiasco Gelato, olives, olive oils and balsamic vinegars. They wanted a store where people could really shop and have a good cup of coffee. Nosh brews different types of espresso: Illy and Mauro (both Italian), and Ethical Bean (roasted in Burnaby). "No frivolous stuff like mochachinos," she says. "Our coffee isn't fancy, but it's right." The biggest surprise for Heather? "We're turning into a coffee shop. We started to grill paninis, nothing complicated, one with meat, one without, and they sell like crazy." They generally have a few oils and vinegars open to taste. Along with the hard goods and coffee, you can pick up baguettes from the excellent JK Bakery and cookies from Sweet Madeira. "Her cookies are *so* good," says Heather.

CAFÉS, BISTROS, DINERS AND NEIGHBOURHOOD JOINTS

Bolo's Ranchouse

838 Main Street   (403) 678-5211
Open daily 8:00 AM–10:00 PM
V, MC

You may remember this long-time corner landmark with the huge south-facing patio as the Sherwood House. In its new incarnation, it's a steak house with Tex-Mex touches. Reliable steaks, grilled salmon, plus pizza, burgers, fajitas (try the cinnamon smoked chicken), chicken mole with a hint of bitter chocolate, braised

bison short ribs with ancho-laced coffee sauce. Weekends they offer slow-smoked prime rib. The regulars love the pub, but the dining room is also comfortable and well appointed.

Craig's Way Station

$

1727 Mountain Avenue   (403) 678-2656

Open daily summer 6:00 AM–10:00 PM; Open daily winter 6:00 AM–9:00 PM

V, MC

> This is simple, old-fashioned road food served by busy, friendly waitresses who assume you want speedy service, coffee with your meal, and your mug topped up. With big omelettes, classic Denvers, pancakes, burgers, steaks and stir-fries and a kids menu, nobody goes away hungry.

French Quarter Café

$$

102 Boulder Crescent   (403) 678-3612

Open Monday–Wednesday 6:30 AM–6:00 PM

Thursday, Friday 6:30–9:00 PM; Saturday 8:00 AM–9:00 PM

V, MC

> A small, bright café with nine tables, where chef/owner Michael Rosso continues his affair with New Orleans culture: jazz, jazz murals, and a jazzy menu with crab cakes, breaded oysters, his own Bourbon Street gumbo, andouille sausage from a local market, fried pecan-crusted catfish and chips. We'd go just for the Louisiana bread pud' with whiskey brown sugar sauce, and the house-made pecan pie, N'awlins style. Ask about cooking classes. Every other Friday, Michael likes to bring in a jazz combo and stay open until 10:00 PM.

The Griesser Spoon

$

104B Elk Run Boulevard (Valbella Meats)   (403) 678-3637

Monday–Friday 8:00 AM–6:00 PM; Saturday 8:00 AM–5:30 PM

V, MC, DEBIT

> Eat in or take out—either way, you can't lose. Roland and Harry Griesser are Austrian trained chefs whose local cuisine is inspired by the wonderful meats of Valbella Deli (V1 p. 56)—air-cured bison and beef, fresh cuts of pork, beef and chicken, or the many versions of knackwurst, bratwurst and jagdwurst. Try their chicken pot pie, the tourtiere made with venison and buffalo, the souvlaki, the sandwiches stuffed with deli meats. There's an in-house bakery for breads, flans and fruit pies, including strawberry rhubarb in season. There are a few tables if you want to eat in, but most people take it home. Custom catering, take-out platters; fondue and raclette can be arranged, plus the turducken, in season. No kidding.

Rocky Mountain Flatbread Company

838 10th Street   (403) 609-5508

Daily 5:00 PM–10:00 PM

V, MC, AE, DEBIT

Partners Ralf Wollmann, Domenic and Susanne Fielden and John MacLean opened the Rocky Mountain Flatbread Company in May of 2004. They use a combination of organic flours from BC in their dough. It's a bit like pizza, but the dough is made without oil—just flour, yeast, salt and water. This restaurant's menu lists half a dozen or so flatbreads, daily pastas, salads, soups and specials. We saw some of our favourite farmers named here, like Hoven Farms beef and Sunworks chicken. We loved the Parma—thin slices of Parma ham with mango, sweet paprika, brown mushrooms and ripe avocado.

Frozen Rocky Mountain Flatbreads are available at Planet Organic in Calgary and Edmonton; Marra's and Nutter's in Canmore and Keller's in Banff.

Rose and Crown

749 Railway Avenue   (403) 678-5168

Open 11:00 AM–2:00 AM

V, MC, AE, DEBIT

We like the warm comforts of the well-established pub; the dining room, with its wonderful mountain view; and on hot summer days, there's the shaded outdoor patio on the bank of Policeman's Creek. The food is casual, but the professional kitchen elevates it well beyond the freezer-to-fryer pub grub we so often find in resort towns. Steak and kidney pud' is made the proper English way, with puff pastry on top and a splash of Guinness in the gravy. There's a memorable steak sandwich on crusty, thick-cut bread, the local beef finished with fried onions and mushrooms, just the way we like it. There are more than a dozen beers on tap. We haven't sampled the Sunday brunch, but the chef promises eggs Benny done a dozen ways.

Summit Café at Cougar Creek Crossing
$

102–1001 Cougar Creek Drive   (403) 609-2120
Open daily 6:30 AM–6:00 PM
V, MC

> This small café is packed at breakfast and lunch when the locals park their bikes
> and come in for omelettes, breakfast burritos, eggs any way you want them. The
> homemade nine-grain molasses bread makes a killer sandwich. Kids and seniors
> get special treatment—we love the Mickey Mouse waffle. Outdoor tables for
> sunny days, a fireplace when it's chilly. Good coffee. Note: Food from the grill is
> available 7:00 AM–4:00 PM only.

BIG NIGHTS, SPLURGES & CELEBRATIONS

Chef's Studio Japan
$$

108–709 Main Street, entrance in the alley   (403) 609-8383 R
Open Monday–Friday 11:30 AM–2:00 PM; 5:30 PM–10:00 PM
Saturday, Sunday 12:00 PM–2:30 PM; 5:30 PM–10:00 PM
V, MC, AE, DEBIT

> Not your usual sushi house. This tucked-away spot offers some creative twists on
> classic technique. There's a good variety of nigiri sushi; various rolls and cones;
> plus tempura, seafood hot pots, teriyaki and sukiyaki. The issunboushi is a special
> dinner for two with a bit of everything, served on a double-tiered dish. A child's
> menu is available—rare, in a Japanese restaurant.

Copper Door
$$

726 9th Street   (403) 678-5233 R
Open daily 5:00 PM–10:00 PM
V, MC, AE

> Chef/owner Chris Dmytriw makes fresh bread daily—a great beginning. He uses
> nothing but the best AAA beef for his steaks. Look for herb-roasted leg of lamb,
> wild game, and fresh fish.

Murrieta's Grill
$$

200–737 Main Street   (403) 609-9500 R
Open Monday–Thursday 11:00 AM–11:00 PM
Friday, Saturday 11:00 AM–1:00 AM; Sunday 11:00 AM–10:00 PM
V, MC, AE, DEBIT

> Murrieta's windows are open wide on fine days, and the aromas of good food

waft over the street below. This upstairs restaurant is a handsome, white-table-cloth dining room with high ceilings, and tall wooden wine cupboards forming one wall. They do well with seasonal and regional specialties—a buffalo ribeye with an inventive lingonberry hollandaise; elk shank with blackberry demi-glace and roasted root vegetables; thick steaks; double-cut pork chops. A recent menu included prawns with vanilla saffron butter, roasted jumbo tiger prawns with two sauces, salmon, Arctic char or ahi tuna. Flatbreads are baked in house. Good wine list, exceptional selection of single malt Scotch, live jazz on weekends.

$$ **Quarry Bistro**
718 Main Street   (403) 678-6088 R
Open Wednesday–Friday 11:30 AM–2:30 PM; 5:00 PM–10:00 PM
Saturday, Sunday 9:00 AM–2:30 PM; 5:00 PM–10:00 PM
V, MC

Brother and sister duo David and Naomi Wyse have a handle on local/regional ingredients, and David's seasonal dishes reflect his fondness for Italian/French cooking. We love the roasted red pepper sandwich layered, Italian style, with asiago, grilled eggplant and basil-laced mayo; the cranberry ricotta ravioli with duck confit and sage butter; the portobello mushroom with goat cheese, Swiss chard and thin-sliced beet chips. The excellent service in a contemporary setting is complemented with the well-rounded wine list with some interesting, unusual choices. Coveted seating in summer is on the street-side patio.

$$ **Sage Bistro**
1712 Bow Valley Trail   (403) 678-4878 R
Open daily summer 8:00 AM–10:00 PM
Open daily winter 5:00 PM–9:00 PM
V, MC, AE, DEBIT

Sage celebrates regional Canadian ingredients, changing the menu seasonally, offering the best and freshest. Look for local free-range eggs, venison meatloaf with mushrooms, double-cut pork chops, braised bison shanks. Provenance is important to chef Jason Rennie, and local sources are often named on his menus. Still, he doesn't build fences around his cuisine, and you'll find very good Australian lamb, ahi tuna, Arctic char. For dessert, the delicate maple crème brulée is divine. It's a warm, comfortable room, and in summer the flowery deck has a fine view of the surrounding peaks.

Bella Crusta (403) 609-3366 (p. 57); Crazyweed (403) 609-2530 (p. 58); Chez François (403) 678-6111 (p. 59); Des Alpes (403) 678-6878 (p. 59); Musashi (403) 768-9360 (p. 58); Marra's (403) 678-5075 (p. 57); Zona's (403) 678-6111 (p. 59)

◎   BANFF

PANTRY

The Fudgery
215 Banff Avenue   (403) 762-3003
Open daily 9:00 AM–11:00 PM
V MC, DEBIT

> We love this place, especially their cashew log, their turtle fudge, and their 19 other varieties of pure butter-cream-sugar fudge. Candy lovers like us go crazy here. There's a big selection of chocolate candies, hard candies, caramels. Ice cream too. Yum.

RESAURANTS

$$ **Typhoon**
211 Caribou Street   (403) 762-2000 R
Open daily 11:30 AM–3:00 PM; 6:00 PM–1:00 AM
V, MC, AE, DEBIT

> Stephane Prevost and Kate Lane are creating some of the most vibrant, sensual restaurants in Banff. Take Typhoon, an intimate spot offering a pan-South Asian menu—curries, vindaloo laksa, pho—and doing it superbly. The green papaya salad with sweet/sour flavours and crisp textures makes a delicious lunch. The mango pudding will make you whimper for more. The wine list is superb. Choose from a whack of Rieslings and Pinot Gris, both new world and old, chosen to work with the intricate and layered flavours of the food. The room is gorgeous— the colour and textures take you out of the Rockies for a brief tropical moment. Kate's exuberant paintings finish the room.

Café Soleil

208 Caribou Street   (403) 762-2090 R

Open 7:00 AM–10:00 PM

V, MC, AE, JCB, DEBIT

It's another Prevost/Lane collaboration, right across the street from Typhoon.

This time, the scene is the south of France. Stone floors, bistro tables, wrought iron flourishes, and more of those vibrant paintings. The menu is a large

selection of tapas, panini, thin-crust pizza, and a few pastas. The grilled chicken with fig was perfectly prepared, the figs lending a sultry sweetness to the grilled flavours. Two excellent salads—roasted fennel, orange and date, and curly endive with blue cheese and walnut. The spaghetti puttanesca was as full-on as could be, with kalamata olives, anchovies, garlic and salty capers leading the charge. Larger dishes are served in the evening: lamb tagine, beef tenderloin with gorgonzola sauce, roast chicken with lemon olive sauce. For dessert try the pear clafouti: fresh pears, buttery pastry. The wine list features flavours of the south—Syrah, Marsanne, Viognier, Sangiovese, Tempranillo. There are over 25 wines by the glass, primarily

from the Mediterranean basin; Spain, Italy France. A nice touch: sherry served in a copita, the traditional tasting glass in Spain.

MukaMuk in the Juniper

100 Timberline Road, bottom of Mt. Norquay Road   (403) 862-4900 R

Open 5:00 PM–9:00 PM

V, MC, AE, ENR, JCB, DEBIT

Muk a Muk (meaning "food" or "to eat" in Chinook Jargon) is an experience in indigenous aboriginal foods and cooking techniques in the old Timberline Lodge. Chef Tom Bielec uses local meats, fish and game.

Luxe wining and dining

The 13th Annual International Festival of Wine and Food, at the Fairmont Banff Springs. Savour two full days of classic tastings, seminars and distinctive flavours of fine cuisine. To book, or for more information, go to www.fairmont.com.

Christmas in November at Fairmont Jasper Park Lodge is an annual festival of food, wine, and entertaining personalities with a holiday theme. Call (780) 852-3301 or visit www.fairmont.com.

Culinary and Wine Weekend, now called The Epicurean Food & Wine Festival, at Fairmont Jasper Park Lodge happens every February, a midwinter celebration of good food and drink. Cooking demos, wine tastings, kitchen tours. Call (780) 852-3301 or visit www.fairmont.com.

Rens Breur
Food & Beverage Director, Fairmont Jasper Park Lodge

We have a great friend of food and wine in Rens Breur, formerly assistant director of food and beverage at the Fairmont Chateau Lake Louise. Rens is a member of the International Sommelier Guild and a graduate of Amsterdam's College of Hotel and Gastronomy. We love Rens for his interest in Canadian cuisine, in particular VQA wines and Alberta foods. He was instrumental in developing the stellar Canadian Wine & Food Festival held at the Chateau Lake Louise every May. He continues with the excellent Culinary & Wine Weekend held at the Jasper Park Lodge in February.

 JASPER

PANTRY

The Fudgery

618 Connaught Drive   (780) 852-5870
Open daily 9:00 AM–10:00 PM
V, MC, DEBIT

> This place smells sooo good. Blame the fresh candy—double dark chocolate fudge, maple fudge, bear paws (fresh cashews and caramel dipped in chocolate) chocolates and peanut brittle. Watch the waffle cones being dipped in chocolate or caramel, then in nuts—16 flavours of ice cream year round. Yum.

Michael Mandato

Chef, Fairmont Jasper Park Lodge

Michael Mandato came to Jasper from New York via Toronto, and while he was familiar with the phrase "snowed under," it took on new meaning. His biggest surprise, at a resort known for its golf course, may have been the first big winter storm.

"We need two deliveries a week and getting them up the Parkway during the winter is always a challenge."

Mandato is fond of marrying regional products with exotic spices, and introducing new flavours into everyday dishes. "I like the spices of the Middle East with good yogurt, fresh herbs and dried fruits. We're creating our own flavour pastes."

Using a roasted garlic confit as a base, he incorporates spices into it, and uses it as a rub.

For Christmas in November, the biggest food and wine program held at the Fairmont Jasper Park Lodge, he developed interactive food stations. "Instead of the usual buffet, we have condiment stations, so guests can try different combinations—how does an endive leaf taste with honey or tamarind paste? It's fun to do, the cooks and the guests will both learn from it. They have their own greenhouses for herbs and lettuces. The Lodge has begun a chef's apprentice program, and to greater appreciate food sources, foraging has become part of field trips outside the park.

Overall, his guests at the Lodge expect to eat regional specialties. "They love beef," he says. "But we're also using bison, elk, wild boar and game birds like pheasant and quail."

Candy Bear Lair

605 Patricia Street   (780) 852-2145

Open daily 9:00 AM–10:00 PM

V, MC, DEBIT

> The same good fudge as its sister shop (see above), plus popcorn, 26 flavours of ice cream year round, and a wonderful selection of cuddly teddy bears. Bring the kids!

CAFÉS, BISTROS, DINERS AND NEIGHBOURHOOD JOINTS

$ **Bear's Paw Bakery and Café**

4 Cedar Avenue   (780) 852-3233

Open Monday–Thursday 6:00 AM–6:00 PM; Friday–Sunday 6:00 AM–9:00 PM

V, DEBIT

> We mention this again because of the expansion—it's now a full-fledged café. Get here early if you want a bear's paw. Their signature cinnamon pastry is a consistent sell-out. The breads are lovely, the baked goods, squares, muffins, cookies, top-notch. What's new is the soups and sandwiches. One late summer's afternoon we watched a staff member carefully place a hefty lattice-topped just-baked fruit pie in a box, and wondered who the lucky family was. You can buy individual mini pies. They call them tarts but trust us, they're pies.

Bright Spot Family Restaurant Pizza

701 Connaught Drive (beside the Petrocan)   (780) 852-3094

Open daily summer 6:00 AM–11:00 PM; Open daily winter 7:00 AM–10:00 PM

V, MC, DEBIT, PETROCAN CARD

> Bill and Voula Mermingis have owned and operated the 142 seat Bright Spot for 15 years. Breakfast—pancakes, steak and eggs, home fries—is served all day, good fill-up food before hitting the hill. It's a huge menu with 270 items including seafood, steaks, sandwiches, chops, and of course Greek dishes such as flavourful lamb souvlaki. There are 22 different pizzas including our favourite, the Greek pizza, topped with donair meat, feta cheese, onions and fresh tomatoes. And don't leave without ordering the roast potatoes made with oregano, lemon juice and (surprise) a bit of tomato.

Java Jazz

610 Patricia Street (2nd floor)   (780) 852-4046

Open daily 7:00 AM–4:00 PM

V, MC, DEBIT

> We came one morning for coffee and spied the tantalizing array of breakfast pastry just coming out of the oven. Loud music, lots of activity behind the counter. The door was open, we went in. Two behind the counter; one cooking delicious-looking potatoes. We sidled up, all set to order grub.
>
> "Hello, may we order—"The girl gestured at Potato Guy. "Pardon?" he said, music blaring.
>
> "Could you turn down the music?"
>
> "Pardon," he said, clearly irritated.
>
> "Can we have two skim milk lattes, one on ice…"
>
> "PARDON!" he yelled again.
>
> We came back the next day, sat on the engaging patio overlooking Patricia Street, had an excellent (and quiet) breakfast—eggs, toast and potatoes.

Mountain Foods Café

606 Connaught Drive   (780) 852-4050

Open daily 8:00 AM–7:00 PM

V, MC, DEBIT

> John Rieder and Darlene Bailey own and operate this busy restaurant on the main street. It's a fine spot for breakfast before heading off to ski or hike. Casual cafeteria-style menu of hearty dishes: Jamaican curry stew, Mexican potato cake, excellent sandwiches such as roast turkey foccacia. It's skilled homestyle cooking. There are occasional winemaker dinners and evening events.

$$ **Oka Sushi**

Lower level, Fairmont Jasper Park Lodge

Open daily 6:00 PM–10:00 PM   (780) 852-1114

V, MC, AE

"We served 10,000 people in 2003," says Tatsuhiko Okazaki, sushi wizard and co-owner, with his wife Rieko. Tatsuhiko (Oka to his friends) makes it look so effortless as he deftly cuts, rolls and presents singularly tasty bits of fish and rice. You can't go wrong on this menu but be sure to try the unagi, lightly seared eel with rice and a flick of seaweed, and the BC roll with salmon skin. Even the California rolls are above average. You may have to wait to get into this 16-seat gem but it won't be long—it's well worth it.

BIG NIGHTS, SPLURGES & CELEBRATIONS

$$$ **Papa George's in the Astoria Hotel**

404 Connaught Drive   (780) 852-3351

Open daily 7:00 AM–10:00 PM

V, MC, AE, DEBIT

This is a pretty room dominated by a large working fireplace and lots of Jasper memorabilia. Paul and George Andrew started in the hotel business in Jasper in the '20s. The restaurant is now managed by grandson George Andrew. Chef Marguerite Dumont is talented—her soups sing.

Expect bison, grilled lamb, smoked pork tenderloin and the best steaks in Jasper. Choose from a variety of cuts including chateaubriand with all the classic sauces—bernaise, peppercorn, wild mushroom and a delicious red onion confit.

$$$ **Tekarra Restaurant at Tekarra Lodge**   www.tekarrarest.com

Hwy 93 S   (780) 852-4624; 1-888-962-2522 R

Open 8:00 AM–11:00 PM; 5:00–10:00 PM

Seasonal May–Fall

V, MC, AE

Tekarra Lodge is a magical place, especially on a dreamy summer evening when the only sounds are the breeze whispering through the tree tops, the quiet rush of the rivers, and the warm buzz of happy people. The restaurant carries on the romance, seating 90 inside an airy, high-ceilinged log cabin and 40 outside on the cottage-like front porch. David Husereau, with his partner Shauna Piddock, operate the restaurant in the summer. Winter will find David cooking in California wine country, or in Hawaii, or perhaps heading to Japan.

David is well suited to the role of itinerant chef. He loves the different perspective cooking a continent away can bring to his food at Tekarra. So do we. The

Hawaiian experience shows up as a subtle Asian back beat—ingredients like shoyu, wasabi, ginger, partnered with Rocky Mountain bison, caribou, and fish. Upscale spaghetti is made with lean beef, semolina noodles, organic vegetables and braised roma tomatoes. The fish of the day is offered three ways—grilled with fresh herbs, pan fried and served with a sassy peanut sambal sauce or macadamia nut crust on jasmine rice. There's a good, compact wine list, well-selected to go with fish and Asian dishes, put together by Shauna. It's a charming property.

WATERING HOLES

De'd Dog Bar and Grill

404 Connaught Drive (Astoria Hotel) (780) 852-3351
Open daily 12:00 PM–1:30 AM
V, MC, AMEX

This friendly English pub, right on the main drag, is a great spot for beers after a hot hike or a hard day on the slopes.

Downstream Bar

620 Connaught Drive www.downstreambar.com
(780) 852-9449
Open daily 4:00 PM–1:00 AM
V, MC, AMEX

The burgers are top notch on the pub-style menu at this good-looking bar.

The bar is completely non-smoking with a sealed double vented smoking room. Stella Tower and Big Rock on tap. Downstream seats 190 but doesn't look that big with the dance floor. There's an entertaining open mike night every Sunday, plus the occasional name act.

$$$ Stone Peak Restaurant at the Overlander Mountain Lodge

www.overlandermountainlodge.com   (780) 866-2330; 1-877-866-2300 R

Open Sunday–Thursday 5:30 PM–9:00 PM

Friday, Saturday 5:30 PM–9:30 PM

V, MC, AE, DEBIT

> The food speaks of the terrain outside the window and changes with the seasons. Stone Peak is one of the few restaurants where you can find Alberta freshwater fish—pickerel from the deep waters of Slave Lake, baked and served with coriander, and wild walleye with Asian pear zinfandel sauce. Bison tenderloin, duded up with truffles, foie gras and Cabernet reduction is well-prepared, tender, juicy and flavourful. There are several game dishes including Spirit River elk.
>
> Check out the many food/wine packages available throughout the year.

◎ EDSON

$ Blue Jay Café

210 50th Street   (780) 723-3297

Open daily 6:00 AM–5:00 PM

V, MC, DEBIT

> Jackie Biggar's café is the kind of small town joint we dream about. Big, with lots of two-seaters and friendly, homey booths. Breakfast is served all day—there's always a special. Ham and eggs, pancakes, and we love the screw-up: a jumble of eggs, tomatoes, cheeses, peppers. Choose among 20 burgers: chicken, fish, chili, barbecue pork, plus all the usual suspects. Our fave sandwich, the pig and pickle, is a Denver with bacon and dill pickles. You can have a hefty Ukrainian platter, the pyrohy made in-house; a hot sandwich, beef, turkey, hamburger; or classic liver and onions. And yes, there's house-made pie with a good flaky crust. This is hearty, soul warming road food—great for a ski trip or family outing.

$$ Mountain Steak and Pizza

5102 4th Avenue   (780) 723-3900

Open Monday–Saturday 11:00 AM–10:30 PM; Sunday 11:00 AM–9:30 PM

V, MC, AE

> It's fast and handy, with a notable steak sandwich, good lasagne and pizza. Try the fried mushrooms.

Thymes Two

306 Main Street   (780) 723-3350

Open Monday–Saturday 10:00 AM–6:00 PM

Thursday 10:00 AM–9:00 PM

V, MC, DEBIT

This small gift shop carries a good selection of Alberta-made culinary gifts such as Pepperheads Wild Garlic and the original hot sauce. Plus glass, linens and tabletop accessories.

⊚   NITON JUNCTION

Kozy Korner Bakery

North side of Hwy 16   (780) 795-2133

Open Monday–Friday 6:00 AM–6:00 PM

V, MC, AE, DEBIT

A spotless coffee stop en route to Jasper with lots of ready-bake products, plus their own freshly baked loaves. We chewed happily on the baked cheese-pepperoni stick. Soups, sandwiches, breads, muffins and the like.

⊚   ENTWHISTLE

The Riverside Diner

South side of Hwy 16   (780) 727-3650

Open daily 6:00 AM–11:00 PM

V, MC, DEBIT

It's a popular stop for work crews, which explains the mountain of food on the plate. The menu is pretty much breakfast, hamburgers and sandwiches, plus donairs. They make an excellent omelette, perfectly cooked with lots of tasty filling, as was the French toast (made with cream). Breakfast is served with genuine home-fried potatoes—so tasty.

EDMONTON

PANTRY

Fern Janzen
Paddy's International Cheese Market, 10730 82nd (Whyte) Avenue

This is Edmonton's only specialty cheese shop. Fern Janzen and her entire staff taste every cheese in this shop, most of them more than once. "We don't necessarily like every cheese, but we do need to know what it tastes like at its prime, and how it changes as time passes."

On weekends, she always offers four or five cheeses for general sampling, from mild and modest to something more exotic. "Any cheese should be sampled before you buy. It's an expensive purchase, an investment. We sell a lot of English cheese—Caerphilly, port cheddar, huntsman (black waxed, with double Gloustershire in the outer layer and Stilton in the middle). At Christmas, we sell a mountain of Stilton."

Her most unusual cheese? "Stinking Bishop, from England, runny, very aromatic, strong flavour, one of the few soft English cheeses. It's banded in tree bark. "Then there's Bishop's Blessing, a hard buffalo milk cheese from England—it's like a mozzarella on speed."

She also likes Mont D'Or, from France. "It comes in a little wooden case, has an undulating rind, and is so soft you can eat it with a spoon."

WHERE GOOD COOKS SHOP

Barbecue Country
5862 75th Street   (780) 469-9970
Open Monday–Friday 10:00 AM–5:30 PM; Saturday 10:00 AM–5:00 PM
V, MC, AE, DEBIT

> The big new store has an impressive stock of condiments for barbecuing: hot sauces, barbecue sauces, rubs, glazes and marinades, both local and from around the world.

Urban Rustic Gourmet/Olive Me　　　www.urbanrusticgourmet.com
8613 109th Street　　　　　　　　　　　　　　　(403) 988-3281
Open Tuesday–Friday 9:30 AM–7:30 PM
Saturday 9:30 AM–5:00 PM
V, MC, DEBIT

These two businesses share space and occasionally orders, but essentially, Olive Me is an olive business and Urban Rustic Gourmet does excellent small things: hors d'oeuvres, sandwiches, salsas and dips. Geddes Casino's love of world cuisines and travelling is apparent in her fresh, uncomplicated approach to food at Urban Rustic Gourmet. Personal chef and meal planning service, including frozen meals for a variety of diets—Weight Watchers, South Beach, Zone and medical conditions. Isabelle Fontaine produces over 25 different marinated or stuffed olives and sells them at the shop, the Old Strathcona Farmers' Market every Saturday and at the Italian Centre. Order olives for a buffet and they come beautifully presented in martini glasses. People will think you're a party genius.

New City Market

May to October
Open Saturday 9:00 AM–3:00 PM

The newest farmers' market in Edmonton is the City Market, a two-block-length of 102 Avenue. The 100-plus vendors include the Deep Sea Chicks, Lola Canola, Holy Guacamole, the Ceviche Express, and the longtime vendors from local market gardens—the Kuhlmans, the Doefs, the Sunworks Hamiltons for poultry and eggs, Bhim's Garden for vegetables and beautiful herbs (fenugreek, cilantro, dill). It also has two major flower sellers, Ukrainian food and a berry vendor.

"In the spring, we have gorgeous bedding plants," says manager Jennifer Gilbert. "You won't want to miss them."

Happy Camel

Old Strathcona Farmers' Market　　　　　　　　(780) 483-0882

Sarah Larsen makes excellent hummus, tabouli, roasted red pepper dip, pita, that sort of thing. The red lentil dip is outstanding. The pita is the Israeli version, softer and thicker than Lebanese pita.

Blue Kettle Specialty Foods

St. Albert Farmers' Market　　　　　　　　　　　(780) 418- 2878

Marcy Mydlak and Carol Olivieri of Blue Kettle Specialty Foods make excellent condiments, sauces, salads and marinades. The Asian marinade for red meat is made with sesame, soy, ginger, onion and garlic. The lemon oregano flavour is ideal for chicken, fish or seafood or lamb. We love their creamy tomato pasta sauce, redolent of butter and summer-fresh tomatoes. The top seller is their chili base with tomatoes, garlic, onion and spices. All you add is the meat and beans. The line is available at Italian Centre Shop, Barbecue Country, Paddy's, From the Good Earth, Grapevine Deli (St. Albert) and Baskets and Broomsticks (Sherwood Park).

Debaji's Market

9680 142nd Street   (780) 409-9499

Open daily 10:00 AM–10:00 PM

V, MC, DEBIT

Debaji's Market moved into the Urban Fare location in Crestwood Shopping Centre in the summer of 2004. There is large selection of organic meats, fowl and produce, a bakery, an extensive cheese and deli section and over 150 prepared meals to go, ideal for busy people.

Cally's Teas

8610 99th Street   (780) 432-3294

Open Tuesday–Saturday 11:00 AM–6:00 PM

DEBIT

Cally Slater-Dowson is well known for her exquisite teas. After selling from the Old Strathcona Farmers' Market for several years, she has opened a store next to Tree Stone Bakery on 99 Street. One of our favourites is Maren's Blend, an aromatic tea of locally sourced organic herbs, pansies, pinks and rose petals. Cally

makes teas for a number of cafés and restaurants around town. You can try the Egyptian Relaxing tea, a blend of organic Alberta herbs and Egyptian camomile, at Culina. Cally stocks tea accessories—pots, infusers, and a selection of things to go with tea—jams, savouries and sweets.

As well, Cally's is a good place to pick up teas from the other Edmonton tea maven, Vitalitea.

Grapevine Deli

10B Perron Street, St. Albert   (780) 459-9849
Open Monday–Saturday 10:00 AM–6:00 PM
V, MC, DEBIT

J. Wagner's excellent deli has charcuterie, bread from Buns and Roses Bakery, Alberta-made and European condiments. The house-made stuffed vine leaves and tzatziki are handy to serve as an appetizer when you're rushed. Check out selected St. Albert Market vendors goodies in the freezer. The spring rolls sold by the dozen are a great buy. Call ahead for large orders.

DeVine Wines & Spirits

10111 104th Street
(780) 421-9463
Open Monday–Thursday 10:00 AM–7:00 PM
Friday, Saturday 10:00 AM–8:00 PM
Sunday 12:00 PM–5:00 PM
V, MC, DEBIT

Ed Fong and partners have created a welcoming urban wine experience as part of the burgeoning 104 street scene. There's real depth in their selection and some surprises—Portuguese and Spanish, lesser known French regions (five wines from Madiran alone), plus extensive Aussies and up-and-coming New Zealand bottlings. Education programs, corporate and wedding services, and there's always something fun on the tasting bar.

Bin 104 Fine Wine & Spirits

5454 Calgary Trail S   (780) 436-8850

Open Monday–Wednesday, Friday, Saturday 10:00 AM–7:00 PM

Thursday 10:00 AM–9:00 PM

Sunday 12:00 PM–6:00 PM

V, MC, DEBIT

> Look for this wine shop as you whiz down Calgary Trail, as it's worth a stop. They're strong in new world wines: California, Australia, Argentina, and Canada (100 well-chosen bottles); plus good depth in wines from Italy, and Champagne. Wine guys Bill Tanasichuk and Chris McKenna run a full program of informative tastings. They know their malts, with a selection of sixty import beers, and fifty single malt Scotches.

Sobeys Hawkstone

4921 184th Street   (403) 441-3502

Open daily 8:00 AM–11:00 PM

V, MC, DEBIT

> Sobey's new Hawkstone store in west Edmonton has an extensive selection of kosher foods: 28 feet of grocery, 15 feet of freezer, 18 feet of frozen meat and poultry. "We are under the supervision of Edmonton Kosher," says Gary Segal, the kosher buyer. "It means we can handle the meat—slice it, make the deli trays."
>
> Hawkstone is a source for tapioca-sized Israeli couscous, and kosher dairy and cheeses from Montreal, Israel, and other parts of the Middle East. Kosher labelling is extremely detailed—a good thing for vegetarians and those with allergies. All of Hawkstone's kosher breads are lactose free.

Pinnochio Ice Cream   www.pinnochioicecream.com

Father and son team Salvatore and Tom Ursino started making ice cream in 1982. Tom loves to work with chefs on custom ice creams, creating a sweet grass bergamot flavour with Jasmin Kobajica at the Crowne Plaza and a chocolate cream cheese sorbet with Brad Lazarenko at Culina. Vitaly Teas delicious liquid chai flavours the chai sorbet. They use fresh fruit purees instead of artificial flavourings, and there is little crystallization due to low overrun (less air introduced during the process). Available at several IGA's, Sunterra and the Italian Centre.

Artistic Bake Shop

6820 104th Street   (780) 434-8686

Open Tuesday–Friday 8:30 AM–5:30 PM; Saturday 7:30 AM–4:00 PM

V, MC, DEBIT

The Artistic has been a south side landmark since Anton and Marianne Schwabenbauer opened it in 1966. Their son Perry and daughter-in-law Katherine bought the business in 1992. "We're still a hands-on bakery," says Perry, who is at

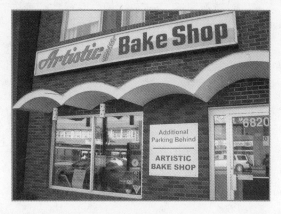

the ovens when the rest of us are still snoring in the feathers. The Artistic handles all the petite fours and friandaise for the Strauss Ball and the Hungarian Czardas Ball. They go a little crazy with gingerbread at Christmas.

Their most important bread is an honest loaf of original rye. "Water, flour, yeast, a touch of salt—that's it," says Perry, who also makes medium rye, Black Forest rye, Westphalian rye with whole soaked kernels, the four pound farmers' rye, and rye buns, as well as six other grain breads and delicious pretzels. On Saturday, try the caraway rye.

Baltyk Bakery

10557 Kingsway Avenue   (780) 428-2207

Open Tuesday–Saturday 9:00 AM–6:00 PM

DEBIT

The little Baltyk Bakery is known for Polish specialties—poppyseed roll, apple cake, cheesecakes. They also bake a heavy rye bread, and their medium rye has sunflower seeds folded into the dough.

Van Sloten's Bakery

6005 120th Avenue   (780) 479-8377

Open Tuesday–Friday 9:30 AM–5:00 PM; Saturday 9:30 AM–3:00 PM

CASH

The Van Sloten family have been bakers for 110 years, starting back in Holland, where baker Art Van Sloten started his career. He's known for his Dutch currant buns, heavy, slightly sweet, stuffed with lots of fruit, and his Dutch raisin bread, with one-third currants and two-thirds raisins. (The buns are also available at Van's Deli, owned by brother-in-law Jake). At Christmas, they do a huge business in traditional pastries: stollen with raisins, almond paste and lemon peel, and their puff pastry almond sticks and almond wreaths, made from scratch. Meanwhile, Art's wife Janna is a cake baker. She's done as many as two-dozen wedding cakes on a single weekend, and you can book a tasting before deciding on your flavour. This year's top seller? Chocolate raspberry amaretto, with chocolate mocha coming second.

Karin's Bakery

641 Broadway Boulevard, Sherwood Park   (780) 467-5809
Open Tuesday–Friday 9:00 AM–6:00 PM; Saturday 9:00 AM–5:00 PM
V, MC, AE, DEBIT

Karin Durand specializes in mini-mousse cakes, 22 flavours available in cream mousse, yogurt mousse or cream cheese mousse, with chocolate and mocha cakes leading the pack. She also does larger cheesecakes and tortes, a variety of small cookies, and the popular no-nuts—small nut-shaped cakes made with sunflower seed, flax, sesame seed and cranberries.

Sugar Arts

(780) 436-3936

www.suargarts.com
Online store

Chef Patricia Bullock and TV and film production artist Jennifer Snyder have combined their experience in a new dessert company called Sugar Arts. They make three things: cupcakes, iced cookies and cakes. The look is whimsical, everything from a cutesy polka-dot number to hand painted athletes or golf tee cupcakes. They make good cookies: sugar and spice, butter, and a rich, almost black chocolate cookie, custom-decorated to fit the theme or occasion. Delectable cupcakes come in carrot, butter vanilla, chocolate devil's food—très chi-chi. They're experimenting with a low-sugar European fruit purée for cake and cupcake fillings. "We've done a lot of one-year old birthday parties," says Jennifer, who also makes house calls for wedding cakes. Their production facility is at Urban Rustic Gourmet at present, though depending on volume and inclination, this may change.

MEATS AND FOWL

Widynowski's Sausage House

4204 118th Avenue   (780) 477-2851

Open Tuesday–Friday 9:00 AM–5:30 PM; Saturday 9:00 AM–5:00 PM

V, MC, DEBIT

> Their specialties are jerky, pepperoni, kubyburgers and, of course, garlic sausage.
> It's all house-made, eastern European charcuterie. They also make and carry
> pyrohy and Ukrainian-style cabbage rolls. This sausage house supplies the Holy
> Cross Ukrainian pyrohy suppers.

Brother's Quality Meats

10145 67th Street   (780) 469-7531

Open Monday–Saturday 10:00–6:00 PM; Sunday 11:00 AM–4:00 PM

V, MC, DEBIT

> This neighbourhood butcher shop is known for it's barbecue-worthy steaks with
> several cuts available daily. They also make fresh garlic and ham sausage, smokies
> and jumbo pork hot dogs. The ready-to-heat dry garlic ribs are a best seller. You
> can also pick up bacon wrapped scallops or crab-stuffed mushrooms.

ETHNIC EDMONTON

One hot summer night, while prowling around Chinatown, we heard Ukrainian music
pouring out of a building, and the thump of dancing feet. One street over, still in the
heart of Chinatown, the Italian bakery was just winding down from a busy day.

If you were trying to explain Canada's multi-ethnic culture anywhere else in the
world, Edmonton would be a good place to start. Little Italy, Little India and a
Chinese/Vietnamese district still called Chinatown lend a distinct cultural and eco-
nomic vibe to this northern city.

LITTLE ITALY

95th Street (Via Italia) at 107A Avenue

Back in the '50s, the late Frank Spinelli befriended and bankrolled the early influx
of Italian immigrants arriving in Edmonton. A community grew up around his grocery
store, the Italian Centre Shop. In wine-making season, the yard across the alley from his
shop always held a few tables for friends, and gallons of homemade zinfandel were con-
sumed on summer evenings over walnuts, cheese and cards.

Second-generation families have moved away now, to greener pastures and bigger
houses, yet the spirit of Little Italy endures along the Via Italia.

Zocalo

10826 95th Street   (780) 428-0754

Open Monday–Wednesday 9:00 AM–6:00 PM; Thursday, Friday 9:00 AM–9:00 PM
Saturday 9:00 AM–5:00 PM; Sunday 12:00 PM–5:00 PM

It's a plant-filled courtyard and house-and-garden shop. Customers sit at the community tavola in the back, sharing conversation with like-minded (or not) strangers, for the price of a cappuccino.

La Dolce Vita

10831 95th Street   (780) 421-0226

Open 7:00 AM–12:00 PM

V, MC, DEBIT

A sports bar on the corner, it attracts an intensely macho crowd who gather for soccer talk and good coffee. Smoke 'em if you've got 'em.

Santo's Pizza and Steak

10821 95th Street   (780) 421-1507

Open daily 10:00 AM–12:00 AM

V, MC, DEBIT

Chef Silvana Cardamone makes her own soups, pasta and pizza. Regulars swear by the steaks, and she makes a killer tiramisu.

Teresa Spinelli

The Italian Centre Shop at 10878 95th Street has always been the beating heart of Little Italy. These days it's owned and operated by Teresa Spinelli, daughter of the late Frank Spinelli.

As Teresa makes her way around the store her father loved, customers constantly stop her to say hello. "These people have known me since I was a baby, sleeping in the store while Mom worked," she says, rearranging a display of figs. "This is home."

After her father's death, Teresa waited a year, then made some changes. She put the shop on computer, and enlarged the always-busy deli counter. At any one time, six white-coated counter-men would be discussing, sampling, wrapping cheese, scooping olives, issuing a running banter with their customers. A seventh was busy making panini-to-order for a gang of young soccer fans, so she instituted a much-needed number system.

"My dad said, 'You can't make Italians line up. They'll never do it,'" she recalls, gazing at the orderly line waiting for service. "But look at this."

Teresa's latest project is a statue of her father, Frank, to be erected across the Via Italia in Giovanni Caboto Park. Naturally, he's seated, cards in hand, playing scoppa.

As we talk, an elderly woman stops Teresa for a chat. Somebody else has a question; a third customer wants another case of tomatoes. She gives each one her full attention.

"I've known most of them all my life," she says. "They're like family."

Sorrentino's
10844 95th Street   (780) 425-0960
Open Monday–Thursday 11:30 AM–2:00 PM, 5:00 PM–9:00 PM
Friday, Saturday 11:30 AM–2:00 PM; 5:00 PM–10:00 PM
V, MC

> An Italian trattoria complete with checkered tablecloths, rush-seat chairs, country-style cooking and a bar across the back of the room.

Tra A Mici
10850 95th Street   (780) 424-8259
Open 7:30 AM–12:00 PM
V

> Sebastian Cerra holds forth behind the bar, the menu chalked on a board above his head. He makes excellent coffee and gelati, thin crust pizza and big sandwiches.

LITTLE INDIA

34th Avenue and 34A Avenue, between 95th Street and 97th Street

It's a long way from the perpetual sunshine of the Indian Subcontinent to Edmonton, yet in two decades, more than 35,000 people have made the journey.

As with Little Italy and Chinatown, Edmonton's South Asian population is dispersed all over town. But for many South Asians, a taste of home is as close as this busy enclave of shops, restaurants and other businesses. Here you'll find a collection of food/video shops for snacking with Bollywood's latest flick, restaurants and sweet shops, meat markets, banquet halls (two more in the works), produce stores, and more than a dozen sari and fabric shops.

Add to this three radio stations, three newspapers, and a total of ten churches, and you're in Little India.

Amrit Bindra in Little India

Amrit Bindra's busy Spice Centre is a vital part of Little India. If you've had a meal in any South Asian restaurant in town, the ingredients probably passed through his store, en route from India, Sri Lanka, Bangladesh, South Africa or the Caribbean.

Amrit arrived in Edmonton in 1989, as an entrepreneur, and spent time in several cities. "Montreal? Language problem. Toronto? Too big. Edmonton? Just right! A developing city. I fell in love with it."

Fifteen days later, he'd bought the store that would become his Spice Centre. "For the first six weeks, I worked the night shift at Canada Post, and opened my store in the morning.

"My customers are from all over the world," he says, pausing by the section he stocks especially for transplanted South Africans, homesick for the familiar packages of Eet-Sum-Mor cookies.

Along with metal serving dishes and the first portable clay-lined tandoor oven designed for home use, he sells musical instruments: sitars, tablas, harmoniums, and all the finery needed for Indian weddings and cultural events. He is heavily involved in the Sikh community and is a partner in the Palace banquet hall.

As the community grows, the stock in Spice Centre changes subtly. Some of the fresh vegetables and fruit, once entirely imported, can now be sourced locally. The aromatic bunches of fenugreek leaves were BC grown. This spring, a local farmer will grow them especially for him.

Miracle on 124th Street

It's been a long time coming, but this area is now a genuine neighborhood for food lovers. We start the tour in the paid parking lot at Mountain Equipment Co-Op. Cross 102nd Avenue to visit the Acquired Taste Tea Company, and the Buena Vista Gelato and Coffee Company, with Bernard Callebaut Chocolaterie next door.

The new Glenora Grill (formerly Nina's) is on the corner, next door to the atmospheric Café de Ville with its lovely courtyard. Cross the street to the Matahari Pan-Asian Experience for noodles and curries, and then to Mangiamo's, for casual Italian fare. Walk north to 102nd Avenue. Turn left (west) to the High Street. Joining the established shops—the Wine Cellar, La Favorite Pastry Shop and Laurie Greenwood's Volume II (for cookbooks)—is the Urban Diner. Across 125th street, is Call the Kettle Black for housewares, joined now by Carol's Quality Sweets. Immediately south are two favourite restaurants, the Manor Café and La Spiga Ristorante Italiano.

Back on 124th street heading north: Rocky River Eatery is a good spot for a casual breakfast or lunch. At 104th Avenue, turn left for tea at Steeps the Urban Teahouse, or head for Carol Amerongen's charming bistro with its secret garden, The Dish and the Runaway Spoon.

Back on 124th Street, around the corner on at 107th Avenue, is Col. Mustard's Sandwich Canteen. A block east is the excellent Blue Pear Restaurant for fine dining. A bit of Greece is still ahead, with the friendly Koutouki Restaurant. Around the corner on 109th Avenue is Hellas Foods, a bustling deli counter and grocery store for everything Greek.

H&W Produce

9261 34th Avenue   (780) 436-7970
Open Monday–Saturday, 10:00 AM–8:00 PM; Sunday 10:00 AM–6:00 PM
DEBIT

One of two big South Asian fresh markets, H&W carries 250 to 300 fresh fruits and vegetables, including all the standard seasonal items. Prices are very reasonable.

Spice Bazaar

9354 34A Avenue   (780) 988-5684
Open Monday–Saturday 10:00 AM–8:00 PM; Sunday 11:00 AM–6:00 PM
V, MC, DEBIT

This cavernous store has canned and dry groceries on the west side, and a large produce market on the east. Prices are low, and you'll find seasonal produce here that isn't available elsewhere—giant squash and pumpkins, yams, soursop, bread fruit, other case lots of tropical fruit. They also handle a small stock of traditional South Asian cooking pots.

Lahore Sweet House

9348 34th Avenue   (780) 435-9419

Open daily 11:30 AM–9:00 PM

V, MC, DEBIT

Juneid and Zehra Quraishi have about two dozen different sweets available at all times, including eight different flavours of the cooked milk fudge called barfi. They also make patisa (sweet pastries), ras gula (sweet cheese poached in syrup), gulab jaman (fried cheese in syrup), and crumbly milk cake.

Their most popular sweet is jalabi, a sort of pretzel dipped in syrup. "We make it every day," says the smiling clerk. "It's cheap and it's so yummy."

FROM VOLUME ONE WE STILL LIKE

JB Cash and Carry Supermarket (780) 468-9455 (p. 98); the Spice Centre, (780) 440-3334 (p. 98); the Maurya Palace, (780) 468-9500 (p. 132)

CHINATOWN

For decades, a tiny Chinatown huddled around 97th Street and Jasper Avenue, near the big Friendship Gate. Eventually an influx of Vietnamese, Thai and Cambodian immigrants opened restaurants and food shops further along 97th Street, tweaking the identity of old Chinatown.

Grocery stores, restaurants, bakeries and barbecue shops define this as a food lover's neighbourhood. The red street lamps add a festive Old China look, enjoyed by tourists but resented by cool westernized youth from the Chinese community. Yet many restaurants and shops in the district maintain small active shrines, strategically positioned to ward off evil at the door.

Patrick Chan once worked in his family's restaurant, the original Tan Tan on 96th Street and Jasper. Eight years ago he opened his own restaurant, Noodle Noodle, and hired two sets of cooks—Chinese for daily dim sum, Vietnamese for the broader menu.

"Things have changed," he says. "There's a real mix here." David Vu, of Hoang Long Restaurant, also feels the changes, "This area is like a village." His Vietnamese salad rolls are served beside Japanese sushi and Chinese spring rolls at parties around town.

As with our other ethnic neighbourhoods, some places don't change: the Pagolac, the Golden Bird, the old Taipan Café, the Hong Kong Bakery with its custard tarts, moon cakes, and cream-filled tortes. Others are up and down like a yo-yo, closing, reopening, changing names and ownership without missing a beat.

There are dim sum places all over Edmonton, but it's fun to be in Chinatown on a Sunday morning, lining up for a table at the Mirama or Noodle Noodle, and spending a couple of hours drinking tea and nibbling on har gau and sui mai. In the same neighbourhood, there are a dozen Vietnamese places to drink strong, filtered coffee, or you could stop at the Bubble King or the Tea Bar Café for a Taiwanese bubble drink.

Grocery shopping in Chinatown? The Lucky 97 and United Grocers have bins of jackfruit and durian; cooking pots and joss paper, herbal teas and ginger pickle, tamarind juice and bamboo tips.

Some of the smaller, older shops look a bit tired these days. There's tough competition in bigger, glitzier stores in other parts of town. But the flavour of Chinatown is still here, where the clock has slowed down a little, where someone still leaves offerings in small dusty shrines, and where a fresh fish is still a swimming fish.

OTHERS WE LIKE

The Garden Bakery and Restaurant (780) 423-7828, the Hong Kong Bakery (780)429-3838, Vinh Fat Food Products (780) 426-3656, the Lucky Town Market (780) 990-1500. **From Volume 1** we still like: Tung Lam (780) 423-0967 (V1 p. 97) the Lucky 97 (Dong Phuong) Oriental Market (780) 424-8011 (V1 p. 95) and Hiep Thanh Trading (780) 424-6888 (V1 p. 94).

DINING OUT IN EDMONTON
CAFÉS, BISTROS, DINERS AND NEIGHBOURHOOD JOINTS

Spago
$

12433 97th Street   (780) 479-0328
Open Monday–Thursday 10:00 AM–9:30 PM; Friday 10:00 AM–11:30 PM
Saturday 4:00 PM–12:00 PM; Sunday 10:00 AM–8:30 PM
V, MC, DEBIT

Come hungry. This is amazing food and the portion size is legendary. There are several Portuguese specialties on the must-have list. Bacalhau a bras is cod with

Brad Smoliak cooks   (780) 893-1733

Brad Smoliak learned to cook in Greece. While travelling there as a student he found himself running a hotel and cooking in the taverna. He's worked with the Earl's chain, was head chef at Normand's and was cofounder/partner of the Hardware Grill.

Now, as a personal chef, he offers in-house cooking classes and catered events. "I'm thrilled to be doing my own thing. It works better with my family.

"People choose the menu they want. Thai is popular; so are do-ahead menus for big nights like New Years Eve." Brad cooks and his wife Leanne bakes. Their barbecue rubs and baked goods are available at the New City Market in the summer.

potatoes, sautéed onion and garlic, with a crispy/soft texture and earthy flavour. The fisherman's platter: half a steamed lobster, a grilled beef strip loin, halibut, and a combination of other seafood—mussels, clams, prawns, scallops and calamari, prepared in a rose sauce with rice. Note: this is for one person.

Or, have steak, pan-fried with roasted garlic in a clay casserole with the can't-stop-eating-them round-cut fries and a fried egg on top. The all-day Sunday brunch (they open early to accommodate the big after church crowd) is a collection of traditional Portuguese dishes with some Canadian cooking as well. We love their feijoada (say fajwdah) a pork and bean stew similar to cassoulet from the south of France. Portugal's wine-making renaissance is evident in some of the new selections on Spago's wine list. Maria Nobre's restaurant is a family affair. Her son-in-law Jason Ponto is her sous chef, daughter Carla works the floor and her husband occasionally tends bar.

The Cooking Queens of Whyte Avenue

Two sisters, Julia Kundera and Zofia Trebaczkiewicz, have a long history cooking on Whyte Avenue, having opened their first restaurant in 1987. "Mosaics was the first non-smoking restaurant in Edmonton," says Zofia, proudly.

They have since gone on to own and operate several restaurants and even a bar. They had purchased the Bagel Tree location before a disastrous Whyte Avenue fire leveled the entire corner.

From the ashes rose Flavours Modern Bistro, a sleek, atmospheric room, possibly home to ... a ghost? "Things happened during construction that led us to believe we had company," said Zofia. "A presence. We even called in a priest. Whoever she is, she's still here, and we think she's ok."

Flavours has a big kitchen. They already made everything from scratch, and now they can do more involved cooking, make in gnocchi and ravioli.

"On a Saturday morning at our other restaurant, Two Rooms Café, there's a real feeling of community. We want Flavours to have the same feeling," says Zofia. "Our kids were raised in the kitchen. When either of us was home on maternity leave, we'd do the baking there."

Zofia's favourite thing to cook? "The lentil soup. It smells so good. It brings people in, and they start to chat ... how do you make it? It's interactive."

$ **Two Rooms Café**
101–10324 82nd (Whyte) Avenue
Open summer Monday–Friday 9:00 AM–12:00 PM; Saturday 8:00 AM–10:00 PM
Sunday 10:00 AM–9:00 PM; Open winter Monday–Friday 9:00 AM–9:00 PM
VISA, MC, DEBIT

Two Rooms Café manages to produce rib-sticking soul food out of a closet that masquerades as a kitchen. We love the Indian spiced tofu scramble for breakfast, along with the legendary muffins, often made with Dad's own sour cherries or a customer's garden raspberries. The warm prosciutto sandwich with spinach, feta, red pepper and tomatoes is a standout for lunch, as is the lentil soup, their potato pancake goulash and the black bean vegetarian chile. Desserts are homey and flavourful, big enough to share. The carrot cake defines the category.

Flavours Modern Bistro

10354 82nd (Whyte) Avenue   (780) 439-9604
Open daily 11:00 AM–11:00 PM
V, MC, DEBIT

Winter 2004 saw the opening of another restaurant by Julia and Zofia, the cooking sisters: Flavours, an opening delayed years by the fire that wiped out several businesses in the heart of Old Strathcona. Expect a selection of toothsome sandwiches and a modern, locally sourced tweaking of classic bistro dishes: braised lamb shanks with white bean and lentil ragu, duck confit salad with summer greens, five spice and root vegetable pot pie. Standouts from the most recent menu include a wild boar BLT and bison osso buco served with fresh herb buttered noodles. The restaurant has large garage-door windows. In good weather, diners can spill on to the avenue and survey the always colourful scene.

The Blue Plate Diner

$$

10145 104th Street   (780) 429-0740

Open Sunday–Thursday 9:00 AM–9:00 PM

Friday, Saturday 9:00 AM–11:00 PM

V, MC AE DEBIT

> Rima Devitt and John Williams, formerly of Zenari's on First, have opened a restaurant that pays homage to the American diner tradition. It's a fun menu with the flavours of the southwest and of the American south. Try the Virginia breakfast (two eggs, corn cakes, apple butter and a grilled pork chop) at brunch. The cooking by Michelle Hobbs is robust, and reflects a variety of influences.

> "My mother is Asian, and learned to cook western food from a magazine. And I love the food of Northern Italy." The meatloaf, tuna melt and cheeseburger are top notch. Hotcake lovers will go for the scratch buttermilk pancakes and the desserts are rich and calorie-laden, as all good diner food should be. Don't miss the house special—apple-jack pie made with Jack Daniel's whiskey.

Blue Chair Café

$

9624 76th Avenue   (780) 989-2861

Open Wednesday–Friday 11:30 AM–2:00 PM; 5:00 PM–close

Saturday, Sunday 11:30 AM–3:00 PM, 5:00 PM–close

V, MC, DEBIT

> A new spot to try global dishes—Thai curries, goat curry, fruit salad, prawns in coconut curry, other things from owner Harold Wollins travels. Live music Thursday nights and Saturday afternoon, and occasional acts on Saturday nights.

Sankyu Modern Japanese Cuisine

$$

15041 Stony Plain Road   (780) 484-1661

Open Monday–Friday 11:00 AM–9:00 PM

Saturday 4:30 PM–10:00 PM

Sundays, holidays 4:30 PM–9:00 PM

V, MC, DEBIT

> This cool, modern restaurant in the west end is a must for well-crafted, classic and unusual sushi combinations. The food goes beyond traditional, with dishes like pan-seared sablefish with miso mint peppercorn sauce, soya potatoes and asparagus topped with a slow poached egg. Or try delicacies like the fried tofu with sliced tomatoes or miso-seasoned fava beans served in a sweet mirin soya dressing. It's excellent food, artfully presented.

Culina

9914 89th Avenue   (780) 437-5588 R
Open Monday–Friday 9:00 AM–3:00 PM; 5:00 PM–10:00 PM
Saturday 10:00 AM–3:00 PM; 5:00 PM–10:00 PM
Sunday 5:00 AM–9:00 PM
V, MC, DEBIT

Recipe for a successful evening: meet for cocktails and tapas at Culina. The extensive cocktail menu is fun and there is a welcome selection of sherries, ideal with the small plates: curry-spiced scallops on pasta risotto, crab tacos, spicy fried chickpeas. Or have big dishes: flank with blue cheese and chocolate, or richly braised beef. Brad Lazarenko's cooking is confident. There's real effort to serve local free range and organic foods from farmers: banana potatoes from Green Eggs and Ham; Sunworks Farm lamb. Of special note is Sunday family night, a three course menu of whatever Brad happens to be cooking. The modern look of the restaurant and the deceptively simple, casual style is a winner. Expect big wines, on a thoughtfully chosen list.

Padmanadi

10626 97th Street   (780) 428-8899
Open Monday–Thursday 11:00 AM–9:00 PM; Friday–Sunday 11:00 AM–10:00 PM
V, MC, DEBIT

Next time you're hungry in Chinatown, check out Padmanadi, a bright, spacious restaurant. Highlights from the all-vegetarian menu include a zesty spiced eggplant, a mixed vegetable platter and the light yet crispy fried tofu with spicy sauce. The chrysanthemum tea is deliciously restorative.

Leva Cappucino Bar

11053 86th Avenue   (780) 433-5382
Open Monday–Thursday 7:30 AM–9:00 PM; Friday 7:30 AM–10:00 PM
Saturday 9:00 AM–10:00 PM; Sunday 10:00 AM–6:00 PM
CASH ONLY

When owner Antonio Bilotta set out to find the perfect cannoli recipe, he went to the source, the island of Sicily. "I must have eaten 500 cannoli when I was there," he says. The search paid off in the delicate pastry he sells at Leva, near the U of A campus. A snippet of ethereally light dough surrounds a filling made with ricotta and cream, flavoured with dried apricot or pistachio. Have one at the café with a shot of espresso or the traditional accompaniment, a small glass of Marsala. Antonio's mother does most of the baking for the café. The biscotti count is up to eight flavours including cherry walnut espresso, fennel, and a flavourful cinnamon honey black pepper. There are light lunches—three thin crust pizzas (we love the chicken with pesto and artichoke hearts), a really good bean salad with garlic, and several different panini. In the summer, Antonio painstakingly makes small batches of gelati and sorbetto using local fruit. In the winter a great big bowl of house-made minestrone, chock full of vegetables and pasta, does the trick.

Imported beer only: Italian Morreti, Mastro Azzuro and Menabrea, plus Stella and other Europeans. There are interesting wines by the glass, usually from Italy. Perfect coffee.

$$ **River House Grill**   www.riverhousegrill.com
8 Mission Avenue, St. Albert   (780) 458-2232 R
Open Tuesday–Thursday 11:30 AM–2:00 PM, 5:00 PM–9:00 PM
Friday, Saturday 11:30 AM–2:00 PM, 5:00 PM–10:00 PM
V, MC, DEBIT

This smallish restaurant in the big red Victorian is a jewel, serving some of the best food in the region. Menus are heavy on what's fresh, local and in season. Everything is made in house: salad dressings, stocks, soups and desserts. A fall

Willie Whyte
River House Grill

Chef/owner Willie Whyte was one of Fairmont Hotels' youngest executive chefs. We first met him in 1991, when he was the executive chef at the Fairmont Hotel Macdonald. When he and his wife Charlene decided it was time for their own restaurant they chose a big Victorian-style house on the banks of the Sturgeon River in St. Albert, just north of Edmonton.

Willie's food philosophy is simple: use high quality local foods sourced from within a few hours of your restaurant. His menus feature several local products: fetas and brie from Edelweiss (another St. Albert business), pork and chicken from Sturgeon Valley, fish from the northern lakes, bison from nearby Strathcona County. Saturday mornings in the summer you'll find Willie in his chef's whites, at the St. Albert Farmers' market, picking out bunches of golden beets, discussing the spinach crop with a farmer, saying hello to his customers and taking reservations on the fly.

fresh sheet had a salad of organic greens, fire-grilled pear with roasted pecans in a balsamic dressing and Edelwiess soft feta; fine grilled bison rib-eye and chile rubbed double pork chop; other seasonal dishes. The wine list has an expanding selection of VQA with about ten wines available by the glass. Lunch on the wrap-around patio overlooking the river is cool and shady. The main floor patio right beside the river should be complete by summer, allowing for larger festive gatherings.

Wild Tangerine

10383 112th Street   (780) 429-3131 R
Open Monday–Thursday 11:30 AM–10:00 PM
Friday 11:30 AM–11:30 PM; Saturday 5:00 PM–11:30 PM
V, MC, AE, DEBIT

Brother and sister duo Judy and Wilson Wu have once again pooled their culinary energies in a restaurant.

Judy focusses her well-honed palate on a whole new range of flavours and textures. We love the shrimp lollipop, a skewered shrimp in a golden fuzz of shredded filo, deep-fried, served with wasabi yogurt dip. The potato fries are fresh and long-cut, sprinkled with a surprising mixture of salt and crushed star-anise, served in a paper cone with house-made ketchup. Don't ignore the grilled octopus salad with five-spice and tangerine vinaigrette.

Szechuan-spiced beef short ribs are boned, braised in an aromatic sauce, served over house-made herbed gnocchi, so tender they almost melt on the tongue. The Wu's are serving as much locally grown meat and produce as they can, and it's good to see Sturgeon Valley pork, cooked in natural juices, So-Tung-Po style.

For dessert, the sticky rice bombe stuffed with black sesame paste is afloat in a rosy guava mint sauce. This is a truly Asian approach, flavours understated, almost bland, the sweetness subtle, and no great whack of sugar. The wine list has some excellent VQA, and there's a small library of beer—17 of them, from domestic to Spanish to Boddington's and good old Guinness. Dragon well and jasmine pearl tea are both available.

$$ **Urban Diner**

12427 102nd Avenue (780) 488-7274

Open Monday–Friday 7:00 AM–9:00 PM

Saturday 7:00 AM–11:00 PM

Sunday 9:00 AM–3:00 PM

· V, MC

> When your mom told you to eat a good breakfast, she'd have approved of this place. You could go for small and healthy—praline banana bread, fresh fruit and yogurt, or the house granola with fruit and steamed milk. Or you could dive into the protein. Eggs, any style, with multi-grain toast and delicious home-fried new potatoes. There's a tender fritatta, full of spinach, bacon, fontina cheese, garnished with freshly diced tomato, surrounded by multi-grain toast.

> At dinner, there's turkey pot pie, grilled striploin, bison short-ribs with beer and tomato sauce, stuffed pork chop with roasted applesauce. For dessert, we like the apple dumpling. In summer, wait for a sunny day and sit on the back deck, under the trees.

$$ **Oliveto Trattoria**

500 Riverbend Square (780) 435-6411

Open Monday–Friday 11:30 AM–2:00 PM; 5:00 PM–10:00 PM

Saturday 5:00 PM–10:00 PM

V, MC, AE

> Oliveto is the sort of small neighborhood trattoria you'd like to have around the corner from wherever you live: oilcloth on the tables, good smells from the kitchen, a fireplace for cool evenings, and a menu that fits on a single page. It's pan-Italian, with spaghetti puttanesca from the south and veal steak with Chianti sauce from the north. For openers, you could have smoked tuna with capers, red onion, olives and good olive oil—chef Bruce Semak's version of the classic vitello tonnato, sliced braised veal with tuna-caper sauce. In season there's fresh, barely cooked asparagus with prosciutto and thin curls of asiago cheese in a grainy mustard sauce.

> On offer are eight main courses, from a chicken breast with roasted garlic cloves to medallions of beef tenderloin with morels in a marsala-cream sauce, and penne with puréed spinach, cream and gorgonzola. The best dish is tenderloin of pork, cut in scallops and sauced with agro-dolce onion sauce and sprinkled with pine nuts. The house dessert isn't on the menu, but the waitress insists that their tiramisu is the best in town.

$$ **The Bauernschmaus**

6796 99th Street (780) 433-8272

Open Tuesday–Thursday 11:30 AM–2:00 PM, 5:00 PM–8:30 PM

Friday 11:30 AM–2:00 PM, 5:00 PM–9:30 PM

Saturday 5:00 PM–9:30 PM; Sunday 11:30 AM–2:00 PM, 5:00 PM–8:30 PM

V, MC, DEBIT

The sort of cooking that once supported ploughing of fields and driving of oxen continues to keep the Bauernschmaus (which means farmer's feast) bumping comfortably along. We're into big food here. You could start with a liver dumpling soup, or the goulash soup, a beefy tomato base with a couple of chunks of stew beef, potato and cabbage. We love the house spaetzle, more like small dumplings, tasting nicely of butter. Save room for Sachertorte, a light strudel with apples and saskatoons, and traditional palatschinken, a tender crepe with apricot preserves, rolled and served with a vast ruffle of whipped cream.

$$ **La Table de Renoir**

10046 101A Avenue (780) 429-3386

Open Monday–Thursday 11:00 AM–11:00 PM; Friday, Saturday 11:00 AM–12:00 AM

V, MC, AE, DEBIT

It's the flavour of Provence in Edmonton. We love the mussels in their shells, served with perfect pommes frites (twice-fried, thin, delicious) and a garlicy homemade mayo; the prawns baked in a garlic butter sauce with a splash of Pernod for that underflavour of anise; the ratatouille, a proper Provencal vegetable stew. The menu was about to change again as we went to press, but that's always a good sign. Check daily specials for the well-made soups. Yes, owner Pierre Renoir is the grandson of the other Renoir, the famous impressionist.

$$ **Acajutla**

11303 107th Avenue (780) 426-1308

Open Tuesday–Thursday 11:30 AM–9:00 PM

Friday, Saturday 11:30 AM–10:30 PM; Sunday 12:00 PM–9:00 PM

If you're looking for home-cooked Salvadorian or Mexican food, this is the place. We like the crispy chicken flautas topped with lettuce, the enchiladas and the huevos rancheros. Or start with ceviche—chopped fish marinated with lime juice, cilantro, oregano and vegetables. Try the pupusa—a corn tortilla stuffed with meat, cheese and refried beans. The corn tamal, steam-cooked in a corn husk, is served with sour cream, or there's the basic tamal, masa stuffed with spicy chicken and green peppers. They also do a good chile relleno, a spicy chile con carne with strips of beef sirloin in a mildly spicy tomato sauce over rice.

Sapphire

10416 82nd (Whyte) Avenue   (780) 437-0231
Open daily 11:00 PM–2:00 PM
V, MC, DEBIT

> When viewed from the avenue, Sapphire Restaurant and Lounge glows an
> unearthly blue. Walk in and you'll discover the source, a gorgeous sapphire-
> coloured, semi-transparent resin bar, lit from below. White walls, dark wood,
> intimate little tables tucked in corners with flickering votives, white banquettes,
> all lit by that caressing, watery blue. The food is trendy tapas style, salads, finger
> food, good scallops wrapped in bacon served with a light cream sauce laced with
> cinnamon.

Suede Lounge

11806 Jasper Avenue   (880) 482-0707
Open 12:00 PM–2:00 AM
V, MC, DEBIT

> Suede, a hip little spot in the Oliver district, chock-a-block with affluent singles,
> has great ambiance, cool tunes and really good food. Most dishes are small por-
> tions served tapas style, ideal for sharing; sugarcane grilled tiger prawns, chipo-
> tle-braised short ribs, house-made fennel and wild boar sausage, grilled romaine,
> along with a selection of flatbreads and a few sweets—the mango stew with chi-

PHOTO COURTESY SUEDE LOUNGE

nese long doughnuts is worth every calorie. The kitchen is open until 1:00 AM, a big plus in this town where it's near impossible to get anything but fast food after 10:00 PM. The room is a minimalist's dream—steel and wood-topped tables; cream coloured suede and leather banquettes. "We've had one birthday party that started at 9:00 AM with a cooking class in the kitchen, then continued on long into the night." says owner Jeff Koltek.

Yes, there is a TV, showing vintage Ali boxing matches.

$$$ **Boulevard**

10072 Jasper Avenue   (780) 486-5802 R

Open Tuesday–Friday 11:30 AM–2:00 PM, 5:30 PM–10:30 PM

Saturday 5:30 PM–10:30 PM

V, MC, AE, ENR, DEBIT

> Boulevard features classic regional Italian food. If Patrizio Sachetto is in town, he sometimes does special seasonal dishes, like the pumpkin ravioli with sage butter, or the ethereal gnocchi with flecks of black truffle. The menu changes constantly, but look for dishes like Roman-style leg of lamb, stuffed with wine-soaked bread crumbs, rosemary, garlic and mustard. The pasta cartocchio, a Sardinian dish, is seafood and pasta cooked in parchment so all the juices cook into the pasta. The wine list is strong in Italian regional choices that work well with this food. Café Boulevard, for takeaway, open Monday through Friday, 11:30 AM to 2:00 PM.

$$ **The Mikado**

10350 109th Street   (780) 425-8096

Open Monday–Saturday, 11:00 AM–10:00 PM; Sunday 5:00 PM–10:00 PM

South Edmonton Common   (780) 432-4500

1903 98th Street

Open Sunday–Thursday 11:00 AM–9:30 PM; Friday, Saturday 11:00 AM–10:30 PM

V, MC, AE

> We still like the downtown Mikado, and David Okumiya's new location on the south side is stunning. The food is better than ever. As well as pristine sushi and the full palette of traditional cooked dishes, they have a barbecue grill for other chicken, beef and seafood. David invented the famous sushi pizza, now available in three different varieties—salmon, tuna and mixed.

FROM VOLUME ONE WE STILL LIKE

Jack's Grill (780) 434-1113 (p. 123); Il Portico (780) 424-0707 (p. 122); the Harvest Room (780) 429-6424 (p. 121); Madison's Grill (780) 421-7171 (p. 124); unheardof (780) 432-0480 (p. 126) ; the Hardware Grill (780) 423-0969 (p. 118); Blue Pear (780) 482-7178 (p.117); Characters (780) 421-4100 (p. 117); Upper Crust (780) 433-0810 (p. 138); Zenari's Manulife (780) 423-5409 (p. 138); Highlevel Diner (780) 433-0993 (p. 130); Furasoto (780) 439-1335 (p. 130); Bua Thai (780) 482-2277 (p. 129); Packrat Louie (780) 433-0123 (p. 134); the Parkallen (780) 436-8080 (p. 134).

Join top chefs, Alberta food producers and VQA wineries at **Indulgence: A Canadian Epic of Food and Wine** (Slow Food Edmonton Event). Sample masterful food and wine combinations, taste the new vintages and enjoy delicious regional cuisine. Proceeds to the Junior League of Edmonton. For tickets or information, call (780) 433-9739.

Over 70 restaurants take part in **Dine Alberta**, the province-wide celebration of chefs and farmers working together to bring great food to the table. Look for menus that include the best of seasonal and regional dishes. www.dinealberta.ca.

Don't miss the **Country Soul Stroll**, a self-guided driving route through Sturgeon County held each August. This terrific event takes you to a variety of multi-generation family farms, orchards, apiaries and ranches. There's lots of great food: bison burgers at Canadian Plainsland bison; German specialties at Alpine Farm; saskatoon pie at Coronado Saskatoon Farm; strawberry shortcake and hot dogs at Prairie Gardens and Greenhouse. In between snacking visit artist's studios, museums, stables, miniature animals and Western Canada's largest herd of Shetland ponies. It's an ideal way to spend a day in the country. For more information or to pre-book a group tour call 939-4320 ext 222 or visit www.countrysoulstroll.ca. Make it a weekend affair. A number of guesthouses and B&Bs offer a stroll and stay package.

Imagine a country fair every weekend, with field sized board games, clowns and storytellers, exotic chickens, U-pick fruit and juice tastings. That's what you'll find at the **Sprout Farms Fall Fruit Frolic** near Bon Accord, celebrating harvest all September long with different events. A kickoff run, raku and smoke firing by the Sturgeon River Pottery Guild, speakers on growing small fruit, a potato tasting. Events are held every weekend in September. Information and directions: 1 800 676-0353; www.sproutfarms.com.

The Rocky Mountain Wine & Food Festival happens every fall at the Shaw Convention Centre. Stroll, sample, sip, watch cooking demos. www.rockymountainwine.com

ROAD FOOD

Fay's Diner
East side Hwy 2, the Bear Hills rest stop

We'd often driven by this converted trailer near the Bear Hills rest stop on Highway 2 and wondered why there were so many cars in the parking lot. One night, heading back to Edmonton we decided to find out. We ordered burgers and received a double order of gratis wisecracks on the side, and the delish house cut fries—twice fried in the classic method. We watched the boss (not named Fay) work the grill, all the while keeping up a steady patter of quips and conversation. On a hot day, it's a great spot for ice cream with loads of kid-pleasing flavours from Foothills.

 OLDS

The Garden of Eden Okanagan Fruit Stand
Hwy 27 corner
Open daily May–Thanksgiving 9:00 AM–6:00 PM
CASH ONLY

> The fruit comes directly from the orchards, and we've never eaten better peaches. They have everything in season, from tomatoes and corn to several varieties of orchard plums, apricots, cherries, peaches and pears. They take orders for pickling cucumbers and case lots of fruit for jam makers.

Bean Brokers Inc.
Mountain View Shopping Plaza   (403) 556-1069
Open Monday, Tuesday 7:30 AM–5:30 PM
Wednesday–Friday 7:30 AM–8:30 PM; Saturday 9:30 AM–5:30 PM
V, MC, DEBIT

> Connie Harder runs this stylish coffee house. All baking is done in-house, includ-

ing the muffins and squares. This is the spot for an Italian soda or a latte, a rooi-boos tea, a yerba mate, or a dish of Foothills ice cream and biscotti. We enjoyed the details, from the artsy coasters to the tall wooden tables and the comfy seating area. We also like her taste in cool jazz.

Leaf and Bean Coffee and Tea Ltd.
5219 50th Avenue   (403) 556-1881
Open Monday–Friday 8:00 AM–5:00 PM
Saturday 10:00 AM–3:00 PM
V, MC, DEBIT

At the Leaf and Bean you'll find specialty coffees and teas, jet tea smoothies, fresh cinnamon buns. Light lunches are served—daily soup, Montreal smoked meat sandwiches, salads, lots of wraps, and quiche in this freshly redecorated café.

$$ ### Olympia Restaurant
5018 50th Street   (403) 556-5951
Open Monday–Saturday 11:00 AM–9:00 PM
Sunday 4:00 AM–9:00 PM
V, MC, DEBIT

Peter and Mary Michanos run this attractive family restaurant. The usual western dishes are on offer, but their specialty is Greek food. The Olympia platter for two includes almost everything in the house—pita with dip, Greek salad, calamari, chicken pita, moussaka, tiropita, keftethes in tomato sauce, spaniko-pita, with rice or roast potatoes. There's also an appetizer platter. These people try hard.

Little Red Deer Store
North side of Hwy 27

This is a small, well-stocked country store with everything you'd need for a picnic or camping trip, including beverages—having one of the few remaining package licences (that predate privatization) in the province.

Latte, Lefse and Gifts

105 Centre Street N   (403) 638-4008
Open Monday–Saturday 8:30 AM–5:00 PM
V, MC, DEBIT

> At deadline, they were threatening to close this location, pack up their dog, and move their mom-and-pop lefse-making business back to the farm. Phone first to check. This is excellent lefse, hand-rolled and therefore tender. We recommend the plain lefse with butter, sugar and cinnamon, and the warm ham and cheese version is tasty.

Classic Lunch and Cakery

106 Centre Street N   (403) 638-2015
Open Monday–Friday 7:30 AM–5:30 PM
Saturday 8:30 AM–4:00 PM
V, MC, DEBIT

> It's a small, friendly lunchroom run by a group of neighbourly women, and the cooking is real mom-style. We ate a hearty vegetable soup (made with locally grown carrots), an egg salad sandwich, and topped it off with a lemon square made with gelatin and evaporated milk, recipe circa 1950, and still delicious.

The Kickback Kaffe

204 Centre Street N   (403) 638-2800
Open Monday, Tuesday 8:00 AM–5:00 PM
Wednesday, Thursday 8:00 AM–9:00 PM
Friday, Saturday 8:00 AM–10:00 PM
V, MC, AE

> If you're looking for some laid-back nightlife in Sundre, try the Kickback. Meanwhile, they make exotic-sounding coffees, teas, and lunch fare—chicken-cheddar soup, nice big sandwiches, chicken enchilada, a wonderful baked apple dumpling wrapped in the owner's hand-rolled pastry and served with caramel sauce and whipped cream. Now and then there's an almond mocha cheesecake, squares, cinnamon buns, that sort of thing. Some talented local folk usually entertain on weekends.

◎ DIDSBURY

We love the attractively restored main street of Didsbury, part of the Alberta Main Street Program. The program works with municipalities, businesses, and building owners to beautify the community and highlight its history.

$ **The Green Bamboo Restaurant**

1902 20th Street   (403) 335-8899

Open Tuesday–Sunday 11:00 AM–10:00 AM

V, MC

The Green Bamboo offers a full Cantonese menu. There are nearly 20 chicken dishes, including salt and pepper chicken, ginger chicken, kung pao and Thai-style; lots of seafood; several good mein (noodle) dishes. Try the thick, pillowy Shanghai-style noodles in a mild sauce. Spicy dishes are marked with a chili icon. The requisite western dishes are also available—burgers and fish and chips, both with fries. It's a pleasant café in a lovely old brick building; look for the lucky green bamboo plant.

FROM VOLUME ONE WE STILL LIKE

Bricco, Calmar (780) 985-4528 (p. 160); Eco Café, Pigeon Lake (780) 586-2627 (p. 163); Burger Barn, Millet (780) 387-4776 (p. 160); Kavachino's, Lacombe (403) 782-7844 (p. 161); Las Palmeras, Red Deer (403) 346-8877 (p. 164); City Roast, Red Deer (403) 347-0893 (p. 163); Sakura Japanese, Red Deer (403) 341-5502 (p. 166); and our cheese artisans: Leoni Grana (780) 672-1698 (p.159, 195) and Sylvan Star Gouda (780) 340-1560 (p. 160, 196)

THE DAVID THOMPSON TRAIL
FROM SYLVAN LAKE TO
SASKATCHEWAN CROSSING

The Food Lovers hit this trail on a perfect fall morning, when yellow poplars and tamarack trees glowed like candles against the mountains. The heaviest traffic was a herd of frisky goats, skittering across the road to drink the turquoise water of Abraham Lake.

But first there was picturesque Sylvan Lake, one of the busiest small towns in central Alberta.

◉ SYLVAN LAKE

Pier 7
5227 Lakeshore Drive   (403) 887- 0077
Open daily 11:30 AM–11:00 PM
V, MC, AE, DEBIT

> From this big dining room, there's a view of the marina and lake. Good beef, broiled chicken, baby back ribs, lots of fish and seafood. Wednesdays they adopt a nautical note at the buffet with all-you-can-eat crab and shrimp. Thursday there's always a lobster feast. The eat-in or take-out format is a handy one for the beach.

Eagle's Nest Dining Room
Sylvan Lake Golf and Country Club   (403) 887-3030
5311 Lakeshore Drive
Open daily 8:00 AM–10:00 PM; Golf season 6:30 AM–10:00 PM
V, MC, AE, DEBIT

> This handsome dining room and the adjoining Bogie's Restaurant are open to the public year-round, and both the ample Sunday brunch (hot and cold dishes, fruit platters, fresh pastries, eggs, carved meat entree) and the Friday/Saturday prime rib buffets are popular events at extremely reasonable prices.
>
> If you're ordering from the regular menu, they do well with salads and stir-fries, especially the ginger beef. In good weather, patio seating is available.

The Big Moo

4603 Lakeshore Drive   (403) 887-5533

Open daily May–October 9:30 AM–9:00 PM

V, MC, DEBIT

> In Sylvan Lake, you've got your Big Moo, your More Moo, and even your Mini Moo, all on Lakeshore Drive. They do ice cream in a big way, 34 flavours, all from Foothills Creamery. You can also get burgers, fries, fish and chips at any Moo in town.

PANTRY

Cobb's AG Foods

5015 Main Street   (403) 887-2091

Open Monday–Friday 9:00 AM–9:00 PM; Saturday–Sunday 9:00 AM–6:00 PM

V, MC, DEBIT

> Cobb's is the place to stock your picnic basket before heading west along the David Thompson. We like the well-kept produce section, the fully-stocked deli and the in-house bakery. The meat department has everything you could want for a barbecue.

FROM VOLUME ONE WE STILL LIKE

Pete's at the Beach (403) 887-4747 (p. 162)

⊚   ROCKY MOUNTAIN HOUSE

Chef's Dining Room

4523 47th Avenue   (403) 844-4600

Open Wednesday–Sunday 11:30 AM–8:00 PM; Friday, Saturday 11:30 AM–10:00 PM

V, MC, DEBIT

> Lutz Kintzel is a German-trained chef who arrived in Rocky after several years as sous chef at the Banff Springs. He and his partner, Tracy Telford, offer daily soups, sandwiches, pasta dishes and the delicious grilled chicken breast on ciabatta with chile mayo. Their specialty is a little taste of Germany—Oma's pork schnitzel, breaded, sautéed golden-brown with oven-roasted potatoes; bratwurst; or the classic rinder rouladen, tenderized steak with mustard, bacon, gherkin and onion filling, braised, oven-baked, served with red cabbage and spaetzle. AAA New York steak is charbroiled to perfection, and the daily specials

are always a good bet. Leave room for dessert. Black Forest cake, souffle glace Grand Marnier. Tracy's mom, Sylvia Telford, often pops up from Turner Valley with a few homemade pies. "Real apples—not that canned stuff," says Tracy. Note: Lutz and Tracy went non-smoking from the day they opened, which makes a huge difference for food lovers.

NORDEGG

The Coal Miner's Café

In the Nordegg School, Girls' Entrance   (403) 822-2220
Open May–October 8:00 AM–8:00 PM
CASH

The Atlas Coal Mines shut down in 1955, leaving Nordegg pretty much on its own. The big yellow school now houses a museum stuffed with artifacts from the glory days. Two rooms have been turned into a café, run by a local couple and their son. "Mom shuts down in October," he tells you, while warming up a piece of cherry pie. The menu is mom-style: homemade soup; burgers, including the coalminers burger, loaded ($1.25 for an extra patty); sandwiches, cold or grilled, or you can have a toasted ham and cheese. Help yourself to coffee refills—note the collection of pretty china cups and saucers if you decide on one of the loose teas displayed here.

CLINE RIVER

Durn Tree Dining Room

David Thompson Resort   (403) 721-2103
Open daily Mother's Day–September 7:00 AM–10:00 PM
V, MC, DEBIT

Ron and Wendy Killick, their daughter Kelly and son-in-law Wim Smit operate this full service resort with a large dining room. As well as the usual road food of burgers and sandwiches, they offer Alberta striploin steak with mushrooms, sirloin with green pepper sautée, boneless trout with lemon butter, cedar-planked Chinook salmon.

Every morning during the season, the Killicks serve a campers' breakfast in the open-sided summer kitchen pavillion—bacon and eggs, pancakes and barbecued beans. At 6:30 PM the summer kitchen becomes the Rock On Pub, with live entertainment and sizzlin' steaks.

9 THE PEACE COUNTRY

The Peace Country is enchanting, with its poetic, undulating landscape, its foggy hollows among the fragile hills, and its gracious, small town ambiance. We start our road trip to the Peace in . . .

◎ MAYERTHORPE

$ **Mama Gray's Kitchen**

5015 50th Avenue   (780) 812-3535
Open Monday–Friday 8:30 AM–7:30 PM
V, DEBIT

> Mama Gray's daughter, Kelly, owns this tidy, comfortable coffee shop off the main street offering giant fresh cinnamon buns in the morning, house-made soups, lots of sandwiches and wraps, including a tasty Caesar chicken wrap, plus beef or chicken quesadillas. Try the homemade fruit crisps for dessert.

◎ WHITECOURT

$$ **Ernie O's**

Hwy 43 and Caxton Street   (780) 778-8600
Open daily 5:30 AM–11:00 PM
V, MC

> The highway is awash in chain restaurants, but for a basic, good-value steak dinner in Whitecourt, Ernie O's is a good bet. It's big and busy, with a little something for everybody. As well as steaks and ribs, there are heart smart dishes, bison dishes, and the Sunday brunch is a local favourite. Kids and seniors get discounts. Very smoky.

Whitecourt

This is picnic country—13 gorgeous lakes within easy driving distance. Before your picnic, there's convenient provisioning to be had at the local IGA Garden Market—quality produce, deli, in-store bakery. There's the Emerald Garden for Chinese food, and Tastebuds (778-2600) for a variety of coffees and specialty teas with snacks, lunches and sweet things for afters like cheesecake, brownies and cookies. Try the Beaver Creek General Store (778-3636) for homemade fudge and hard ice cream.

◎ FOX CREEK

The Shangri-La

Hwy 43 north side, turn at Petro-Canada, beside Horizon Motel   (780) 622-2288
Open daily 7:00 AM–10:00 PM
V, MC

> Don't be put off by the plain exterior. This is a friendly, family-run restaurant, clean, bright, with careful cooking. Both Cantonese and western dishes are available—hot sandwiches, burgers, the open Denver with lots of onion and celery. On the Cantonese side, the beef and broccoli is a basic, well-made dish, the vegetables still crisp and green. They have a limited number of seafood dishes, plus ginger beef, spicy Szechuan beef, tossed Singapore-style vermicelli, sweet and sour pork.

◎ BEZANSON

Lefty's Café

Hwy 43 (Old Bezanson Road)   (780) 532-8390
Open Monday–Saturday 7:00 AM–9:00 PM
Sunday 9:00 AM–9:00 PM
V, MC, DEBIT

> Having too much fun between Bezanson and Grande Prairie, your faithful trail guides were just crossing the Smoky River Canyon when the gas gauge started pinging ominously. We got lucky and coasted into Lefty's, a small, clean truck stop with gas and homecooking.
>
> "We supersize everything," says Darlene, who isn't Lefty, but does own this place. From the hand-formed burgers to classic versions of

Ice Cream in Crooked Creek

If you're on Hwy 43 between Valleyview and Bezanson on a hot summer day, Mr. Big's Ice Cream Stand beside the Crooked Creek General Store offers both soft and hard ice cream. It's sold from a funky little roadside kiosk that looks positively edible. Open May long weekend, noon to 9:00 PM, although we found the hours to be somewhat erratic.

the hot sandwich with gravy, the steaks, the comforting toast with mushrooms and bacon, this is big food. Homemade pie crust! Oddly, the lemon pie has no meringue. Rhubarb and apple fillings are from scratch.

Adam Ranch	www.adamranch.net / www.albertacountryvacation.com
Bezanson	(780) 814-5618, 1 866-232-6283

The Adam Ranch covers just under 20,000 acres of rolling forested hills and open grasslands along the banks of the beautiful Smoky River. It's a working bison/cattle operation, home to three families, offering unique ranch vacations.

The food is hearty: traditional cowboy breakfast, bison steak barbecues with all the fixin's, and delicious pies made with the local wild blueberries.

Guests stay in the property's original bunkhouses, retrofitted with all the "mod cons." You can work alongside the ranch crew, play ranch polo or perhaps catch a weekend match at the Grande Prairie Polo Club. In July 2000, they were the home for the Last Great Bison Wagon Trek, part of the International Bison Conference in Edmonton that year.

◎ GRANDE PRAIRIE

$$ **The Acropolis**
10011 101st Avenue (780) 538-4424
Open Tuesday–Saturday 4:30 PM–10:30 PM
V, MC, AE, DEBIT

A comfortable dining room with a fireplace for chilly evenings, this is very good Greek cooking. Outstanding spanikopita and hummus. The chef takes special care with lamb, served several different ways—slow roasted shoulder, succulent, delicious, served with lemon-spritzed potatoes; rack of lamb; souvlaki. Or you can have chicken or beef souvlaki with tasty Greek salad. Steaks are available, and if vegetarian is your thing, they have that covered too. There's a non-smoking restaurant and a lounge for the smokers.

$ **Bricco's Café**
101–10006 101st Avenue (780) 513-1313
Open Monday–Saturday 6:00 AM–5:00 PM
V, MC, DEBIT

Dawn and Harley Klatt operate an Italian-style coffee shop right in downtown Grande Prairie. Expect tasty baked goods, muffins, cookies, occasionally pies and cakes. Truly homemade soups, excellent selection of all the coffees, sodas and teas.

$ **Jeffrey's Café Co.**
Centre for Creative Arts, 2nd floor, 9904 101st Avenue   (780) 513-8554
Open Monday–Friday 8:00 AM–4:00 PM
VISA, MC, AMEX, DEBIT

Lance Warkentin's menu has an international flavour, thanks to his travels—bits of Australia and London's vibrant South Asian culture have rubbed off. We like the East India chicken salad—lots of crunch and vibrant flavours here. Also try the spinach salad with seasonal fruit, and the pesto grilled chicken sandwich.

◉　BEAVERLODGE

Soups
908 2nd Avenue   (780) 354-3111
Open Monday–Friday 7:00 AM–4:00 PM
V, MC, AE, DEBIT

Betty Fair's 8-year-old café has a well-deserved reputation for fresh home cooking. Everything is made in house.

"We have bakers come in every morning. The cinnamon knots are wonderful, and usually gone by noon," she says. The chicken sandwich is a big seller—chicken salad with Cajun spices—"Our secret recipe," says Betty. The hot beef sandwich with gravy is another winner. True to its name, they make a terrific pot of soup, different ones every day. Her favourite? "In the fall, I love borscht with all the local vegetables."

Forty seats, casual fare, a cute spot with a patio for summer.

◉　SEXSMITH

A lovely small town with well-preserved character buildings well preserved, definitely worth a short detour off the highway.

Sexsmith Bakery
9929A 100th Street   (780) 568-4434
Open Tuesday–Friday 7:00 AM–6:00 PM
Saturday 9:00 AM–6:00 PM

We watched a steady stream of happy bread buyers pop in and out of this tiny, flour-dusted bakery. We love the homestyle baking here, the raisin-studded Duchies, the jelly doughnuts, the custard-filled buns with a thick layer of chocolate icing like Mom used to make. Everything is baked from traceable grains.

Double B Butcher Shop

9913 100th Street   (780) 568-3861

Open Monday–Saturday 9:00 AM–5:00 PM

> This busy European-style meat shop is next to a lovely old wooden fence, over-grown with vines. They have an impressive selection of fresh meats and charcu-terie, along with several cheeses in a well-stocked deli counter, perfect for pro-visioning a picnic. There are a few tables for soup or sandwich lunch, and the daily specials are chalked on a blackboard.

◎   RYCROFT

Briggswood Country Preserves

4716 51st Street   (780) 765-3180

Open Monday–Friday 8:00 AM–5:00 PM; closed Wednesday afternoon

V, MC, DEBIT

> We're deep in saskatoon country, and the place to buy saskatoon products—jams, jellies, syrups—is Briggswood, a small manufacturer of condiments made with locally grown produce and fruit. We love the hawthorne jelly and the rosehip jelly. These old-fashioned preserves can only be found at this location, although other Briggswood products are readily available in retail shops around Alberta.

Dunvegan Market Gardens

On Hwy 2, 26 km south of Fairview   (780) 835-4459

Open April–September Monday–Saturday 10:00 AM–9:00 PM

Sunday 1:00 PM–9:00 PM

> There are spectacular views along this road, and you can drive down into the beau-tiful Dunvegan Market Garden for bedding plants, corn, strawberries, cucumbers and a variety of other peak-season vegetables, custom pick or U-pick. The origi-

> nal tea room has been replaced by Grandma's Attic, a shop that carries an eclectic stock of beautiful tableware—Watsons pottery in the Suffolk collection, odd pieces of pretty china and glassware. When you're hungry, the General Store sells a dozen flavours of hard ice cream, muffins, coffee and genuine homemade pies, as long as they last.

GRIMSHAW

Johnny's Sausage and Meats
5407 50th Street   (780) 332-2667
Open Monday–Saturday 9:00 AM–6:00 PM

> "Try our wurst—it's the best." Johnny has a sense of humour, and we like that. He also runs a squeaky-clean shop with a great variety of house-made sausages, beef by the steak, quarter or side, and several cuts of marinated meats, barbecue-ready.

PEACE RIVER

Peter Szechuan
9809 100th Street   (780) 624-9582
Open daily 11:00 AM–9:00 PM
V, MC

> The menu in this new location has several Szechuan-style dishes, spicier and saltier than the Cantonese fare that makes up the rest of the menu, here and in most Chinese restaurants in this part of Alberta. Try the Szechuan chicken or the Szechuan assorted vegetables with tofu. Friday and Sunday evenings and weekday lunches Peter runs a popular Cantonese buffet. Lots of combination dinners are available, and if you're settled into a motel and too comfortable to budge, they'll deliver.

Java Domain
10107 100th Street   (780) 624-5557
Open Monday–Friday 7:30 AM–6:00 PM; Saturday 10:00 AM–5:00 PM
V, MC, AE

> In Peace River's only genuine coffee house and internet café, you can have house-made muffins or bake-shop cinnamon buns with your espresso or specialty mug. At lunch there's always a pot of good soup—the cream of potato is a local favourite. Friday is chili day.

Su Casa
9720 94th Street   (780) 624-8262
Open Monday–Saturday 11:00 AM–9:00 PM
V, MC

> Surprise! Peace River has one of our favourite Mexican eateries. In a colourful, casual, smoke-free (yay!) two-room café, we found authentic Mexican food and

homemade sauces with layers of flavour behind the kick, fresh soups and lots of well-made tortilla-based dishes. Try the flacas and the chile rellenos—charred sweet peppers, peeled, stuffed with spicy chicken and jack cheese, batter-dipped, deep-fried but not greasy.

The big plus: Maria's personal favourites, dishes she learned from her mom, are often available as a special, always in small quantities, and the variety changes from night to night. There's a lot of creativity here. The good selection of beer is perfect with this food. Check out the funky artwork.

◎ MCLENNAN

$ **The Coffee Connection**
215 Centre Street   (780) 324-2111
Open Monday–Saturday 8:00 AM–6:00 PM
V, MC, DEBIT
>Here's a comfortable room with a small fireplace for chilly days, a toy box to amuse the kids, and lots of fresh, well-made sandwiches, salads, homemade desserts—chocolate cake, oatmeal cookies, squares, specialty coffees. They'll pack lunches to go. Watch for Sunday brunch from November through April.

◎ HIGH PRAIRIE AND FALHER

This is honey country, and there are some smaller farm gate producers as well as several major honey farms. Watch for signage.

Kemp Honey

Hwy 2, 7 miles out of High Prairie, south side of the road   (780) 523-5367
>It's a relatively small producer who makes your visit easy—he'll explain as much or as little as you like. He sells unpasteurized honey in anything from an 8 ounce

>squeeze-bear to a 15 kilogram (35 pound) pail. Kemp also offers a few value-added products—soaps, insect repellant bars, handcream.

10

◎ FAUST

$ **Antje's Gasthaus**

Open by whim or reservation   (780) 355-3768 R

V, MC, DEBIT

Antje Wolff's lovely garden and charming home make a perfect setting for a restaurant, but as much as she enjoys it, she refuses to let it rule her life. Antje cooks by reservation only—"About three nights a week"—the dishes she loves: beef rouladen, schnitzel, bratwurst, kassler cutlet, red cabbage, sauerkraut, spaetzle.

"I make good chicken soup, but there's not a lot of call for it up here," she says. Antje's can seat 28 people.

◎ SLAVE LAKE

We hear of plans for another attempt at a catch-and-cook restaurant on the shores of this big lake. Watch for it.

$ **Point Steakhouse and Marina**

Off Hwy 88, left at sign   (780) 849-4133

Open daily summer 11:00 AM–11:00 PM

Open daily winter 11:00 AM–10:00 PM

V, MC, DEBIT

If you've crossed the bridge, you've gone too far. This is a handsome building right on the lake, with a fireplace, wrap-around deck, comfortable lounge and a spectacular view. Your best bet on this menu is the beef, advertised as certified Canadian Angus. They serve pie and tea in the afternoon.

The lovely, historic town of Athabasca is a fun Sunday drive from Edmonton. We admire the flower baskets in summer, the frosted trees in winter and the views of the river valley all year round.

$ **Davina's**

4807 50th Street (780)675-3304

Open Tuesday–Friday 7:30 AM–4:30 PM

Saturday 10:30 AM–4:30 PM

V, MC, DEBIT

> High tea in Athabasca includes a full assortment of properly crustless tea sandwiches and a full complement of sweets—depending upon the day it might be almond cranberry shortbread bar, chocolate cake, and of course, scones. Crumpets too, delicious with lashings of butter. Alas, no more Devon cream, so she whips heavy cream to replace it. So yummy.
>
> Need breakfast? Again, it's full English—no kippers, Davina's not Scottish—you'll have bacon, sausage, eggs, tomatoes, mushrooms and home-fried potatoes. Or, boiled egg with toast soldiers!
>
> Delicate crepes are presented in three ways: English style, with lemon juice and sugar; French style, with fruit and whipped cream; or Canadian, with butter and maple syrup. She makes her own bread and buns, so lunch could be a hot chicken or beef bunwich, a good old ploughman's lunch with pickles, cheddar and bread, or the daily special. Two soups are always on offer, plus an assortment of baking—anything from wild blueberry muffins to cinnamon buns. There's a cappuccino machine in this kitchen and loose tea for sale.

$$ **Giorgio's**

4901 49th Street (780) 675-5418 R

Open Monday–Friday 11:00 AM–10:00 PM

Saturday 11:00 AM–9:00 PM

V, MC, AE

> John and Shauna Vamvakakis have owned Giorgio's for six years, and their well-established dining room has become a local favourite. All sauces and dressings are house made, so is the pizza dough, fresh every morning. The Sterling Silver steaks or the marinated flame-grilled pork souvlaki are both good choices. There's always a house dessert, either the cheesecake or a fresh torte. This is a date place—candlelight, soft music, superior service.

Maple Tree Clubhouse

Athabasca Golf and Country Club   (780) 675-7033

Open May–October daily 9:00 AM–8:30 PM

V, MC, DEBIT

> The clubhouse hangs out over the river, offering a splendid view and outdoor tables, perfect for summer or fall days. Steak sandwich, chicken, burgers, and the best fresh-cut French fries north of Wasketaneau!

Riverhouse

5002 43rd Street   (780) 675-5711

Open Monday 8:30 AM–4:00 PM; Tuesday–Thursday 8:30 AM–9:00 PM

Friday 8:30 AM–10:00 PM; Saturday 11:00 AM–11:00 PM

V, MC, AE, DEBIT

> Led by our noses, we climbed the rickety stairs, crossed the empty patio, and fell gratefully into delicious cooking. The Riverhouse is a comfortably shabby room with relaxed service, a small menu and exceptional cooking. They do a fine tourtière, an enviable version of quiche Lorraine with Swiss cheese and ham, and a silky smoked salmon quiche. The Tex-Mex baked potato is a whole meal, topped with ground beef, veggies, salsa, cheddar, and served with two salads. Divine desserts— try the carrot cake, the maple chiffon filled angel food, the sour cherry cheesecake, the pecan pie or the maple-drizzled cheesecake. The partners here make a big thing of healthy food—no hydrogenated oils are used, for instance. If it's available, try the rhubarb spritzer, made with local rhubarb, steam-juiced. This place is smoke-free (yippee) and you gotta love Stewed Roots, the house band, which plays Friday and Saturday nights.

COLINTON

Buffalo J's

Main Street   (780) 675-1125

Open Tuesday–Saturday 9:00 AM–9:00 PM

Sunday 10:00 AM–8:00 PM

CASH

> Judy Barker and John Reiten's 36-seat restaurant specializes in bison dishes. Saturday is bison steak night. The rest of the week there's roast bison, bison burgers, pizza, hamburgers, chicken breasts marinated in the special house sauce, and baked breaded codfish.

☺ DONATVILLE

$$$ **DonatBerry Inn Bed and Breakfast**

1 km east at Donatville on Hwy 63, 16 km north of Boyle   (780) 689-3639 R

> We mention this beautifully appointed inn because they serve a candlelight four-course homecooked dinner, by reservation, only if you're a guest, at $25 per person. People book in just so they can eat here. The breakfasts are bountiful and home cooked, with fresh fruit in season.

☺ GRASSLAND

$ **Wally's Fast Food**

Hwy 63   (780) 525-2522

Open Monday–Wednesday 8:00 AM–8 PM; Thursday 8:00 AM–10:00 PM

Friday 8:00 AM–11:00 PM; Saturday, Sunday 8:00 AM–9:00 PM

> Wally ain't kidding. This place is all about road food, starting with big burgers, drippin' with fixins'. You've got your single or double beef burger, cheeseburger, double cheeseburger, mushroom burger, chicken burger, fish burger. The Wally Burger involves two beef patties, loaded, on a sesame bun. The fries are from fresh-cut spuds, skin on. Poutine is available, so is donair, fish and chips, a kids menu, soft ice cream treats.

☺ FORT MCMURRAY

$$ **Pestos Café**

400–330 Thickwood Boulevard   (780) 714-9266

Open Tuesday–Saturday 11:00 AM–9:30 PM

V, MC

> Karen Ramsey raised the bar a few notches when she opened her lovely restaurant and started throwing around terms like "first cold press extra virgin olive oil" and offering a rustic artichoke dip, caramelized garlic on crostini, mussels in curried bisque, that sort of thing.
>
> Think of pasta tossed with artichoke hearts and crumbled bacon in a gorgonzola cream; smoked duck breast with lingonberry orange compote; rosemary-crusted New Zealand spring lamb; espresso-crusted Alberta beef tenderloin with honey-chili butter and oven-roasted sweet potato wedges.
>
> There's a baker in the house, so breads, pastries and desserts are top drawer. If the raspberry pie is available, you're in luck.

Scott's Meat Shop

Hwy 663, west of town   (780) 623-7743

Open Monday–Thursday 9:30 AM–6:00 PM

V, MC, DEBIT

> Art Scott knows a thing or two about meat. He's been making his preservative-free sausages, smoked and cured specialty meats and fresh cuts for over 36 years. Don't miss the house-made jerky. He also processes wild game.

Snickerdoodles

10105 101st Avenue   (780) 623-2265

Open Monday–Friday 7:00 AM–5:00 PM

Saturday 8:00 AM–4:00 PM

V, MC, DEBIT

> Jim and Rajah Hattum took over this café in early 2003, and with that, Snickerdoodles became much more than a place for coffee and a sweet. They offer excellent scratch cooking—sandwiches, salads and ribs. Rajah's soups are justly famous. Save room for coconut cream or lemon meringue pie.

Hamar Groceries

10111 101st Street   (780) 623-4401

Open Monday–Friday 8:45 AM–8:00 PM

Saturday 8:45 AM–6:00 PM

Sunday 9:45 AM–6:00 PM

V, MC, DEBIT

> For picnics and provisioning, this large supermarket has a good in-store bakery, a deli section, and an impressive display of produce—we found mangoes, melons and big orange papayas from Thailand.

⊚   COLD LAKE

This huge northern lake with its white sand beaches and crystalline water reminds us of a smaller, more northern version of Penticton. Apart from the beach, there's the air-base, known to all of NATO as 4 Wing, where an international roster of pilots comes to train, and the annual Maple Flag (May into early June) brings thousands of visitors to town, filling restaurants, bars and hotels to overflowing.

Hamel's Meats

5209 51st Avenue   (780) 594-5559

Open Monday–Wednesday 8:00 AM–6:00 PM

Thursday 8:00 AM–8:00 PM

Friday, Saturday 8:00 AM–6:00 PM

V, MC, DEBIT

There's some history here: the first generation of this family came to Canada from Normandy in 1656. Arriving in Alberta in 1928, they opened a food shop in Bonneyville.

In 1962, the family opened Hamel's Meats. This wonderful meat market carries lamb, beef, pork and bison, all Alberta-grown. As well, they make their own turkey jerky, beef jerky, excellent bacon and delicious Black Forest ham. Their old-fashioned cretons, a tasty pork shoulder spread, is perfect as an appetizer with bread and a little wine. As well as the meat business, Hamels do some local catering for big events. The location in Bonnyville is owned by Gaston Hamel's brother, Joffre.

$$ ### The Hoof and Anchor

707 Lakeshore Drive   (780) 639-3555

Open Friday–Wednesday 4:00 AM–10:00 PM

V, MC, AE, DEBIT

Dan and Jodie Denton's steak house and lounge across from the Marina has a vast menu that includes all the usual beach fare, burgers, wraps, sandwiches, and interesting appetizers known as beef fingers served with garlic dip. They also have a strong offering of Greek dishes. Don't ignore the steaks. They're certified premium Sterling Silver steaks—the trademark for top quality, well-marbled striploins, charbroiled and always tender.

$$ ### Clark's General Store

701 Lakeshore Drive   (780) 639-4782

Open Tuesday–Sunday 11:00 AM–10:00 PM

V, MC

Picture a historic building with a counter from an old Red and White, bright red stools, black and white tile floors. They've nailed the ice cream parlor look, and they do an admirable version of beach food: barbecued chicken, steak, burgers, salads, poutine. We like the tiger prawn Caesar salad, the bruschetta, the charbroiled chicken garden salad. Among the near-dozen burgers, try the onion lovers burger—a six-ounce all-beef on a Kaiser, garnished with fresh raw and sautéed sweet onions. A slice of good cheddar is melted over top. Comes with fries, or onion rings, or a freshly made salad. Ingredients at Clark's are first class, and that makes all the difference.

There's a small brick patio in front, lots of indoor seating. Service here is by friendly helpful locals who are proud of their town.

Mediterranean Grill
Lakeshore Drive   Unlisted number
Dinner only
CASH ONLY

This grill has two small rooms, a patio for summer dining and a short but tasty menu. Chicken souvlaki comes with Greek salad, pita bread and hummus; medallions of pork tenderloin are cooked with mushrooms in a wine sauce, and have Caesar salad and garlic bread on the side. At deadline this business appeared to be still settling in, but any restaurant that grows its own herbs in big pots gets our vote for trying harder.

Harbour House Tea Room
615 Lakeshore Drive   (780) 639-2337
Open Monday–Saturday 11:00 AM–10:00 PM
V, MC

This is one of several charming waterfront B&Bs, and they're now making full use of their large breakfast room by offering lunch and dinner. At lunch, expect garden or Caesar salad, soup of the day, spinach lasagna or a variety of creative meal-sized sandwiches—ham and honey mustard with cheese, Italian meatloaf bruschetta and cheese, a chicken quesadilla. Dinner is more of the same, with a selection of appetizers (sticky wings, pita with hummus, bruschetta, hot artichoke dip, deep-fried Asian

Cookin' the Catch

It's a crying shame that with all the deep, cold lakes in this part of the province, it's almost impossible to eat local freshwater fish in a restaurant, and not easy to find in a supermarket. Where does it go?

"To New York," said our source. Local fish markets apparently don't have much access to the abundant fish in these waters, so the fish-hungry tourist industry eats Captain Highliner.

But if you go fishing and get lucky, here's an idea: Clark's offers something they call Dinner Your Way. For $12 per person, with advance notice and a reservation, they'll cook your fish or game for you, and serve it with all the appropriate go-withs, including vegetables, salad and sauces as appropriate.

spring rolls) plus the daily stew, and a daily special. During the day, they serve espresso and other Italian coffees, Tazo teas and soft drinks.

Community Fish Fry

For tickets, call 780 594-4747

The annual Cold Lake Community Fish Fry is held every year in early August, at the Marina. The fish is cooked on the barbecue and served buffet-style, with all the trimmings: potato, three salads, lemons, tartar sauce and dessert, but it's the fish that makes the event run. Look for two favourites—big, firm whitefish, or northern pike, both fresh-caught from this deep, cold lake. This event grows by leaps and bounds—last year they served 400-plus.

$ **Bear Ridge Café**
4–1020 8th Avenue (780) 639-3633
Open Monday–Friday 8:00 AM–10:00 PM
Saturday 9:00 AM–10:00 PM; Sunday 12:00 PM–5:00 PM

> We mention this because it's an internet café with high-speed internet, CD burners, fax, printer and copier. To sustain you while you work, they offer a variety of teas and Italian coffees plus other light fare—soup and sandwiches, or muffins, pies and calorific snacks for when the going gets tough. Thursday night is wing night.

WATERING HOLES

Marina View Hotel
902 8th Ave (780) 639-3261
Open 11:00 AM–1:00 AM

> The Marina View has a huge outdoor patio with a primo view of the waterfront scene. During Maple Flag, when every other outdoor seat along the strip is occupied, you might still squeeze in here.

Joe's Bar and Grill
Canex Centre, on the airbase

Want to rub shoulders with the military? Better yet, the international, crème de la crème, airborne military? The International Test Pilots School operates out of this base—note the collection of international squadron insignia on the way in to the lounge.

During Maple Flag, this has to be one of the most entertaining bars in North America. Civilians are welcome at Joe's, and if you don't have a good time it's your own fault.

Overnight Truck Stop Cinnamon Buns

¼ cup (50 mL) sugar
½ cup (125 mL) warm water
1 pkg. active dry yeast
½ cup (125 mL) milk
3 tablespoons (45 mL) butter
1 teaspoon (5 mL) salt
2 eggs
4 cups (1 L) all-purpose flour, approx.

Cinnamon filling:
¾ cup (175 mL) soft butter
1 ½ cups brown sugar
½ cup chopped walnuts
½ cup raisins
1 tablespoon (15 mL) cinnamon

Make the sponge: In a large bowl, dissolve 1 teaspoon (5 mL) sugar in warm water. Stir in yeast and let stand until it froths. Heat milk, remaining sugar, salt and butter until butter melts. Cool, and beat in the eggs. Stir into yeast mixture. Gradually beat in 1 cup flour until smooth. Beat in remaining flour with a wooden spoon—dough will be sticky and soft.

Turn onto a lightly floured board and knead until elastic and smooth. Return to large bowl, oiling the bowl first. Cover with plastic and place in fridge at least 8 hours or overnight to rise.

Punch dough down. On a lightly floured board, roll into a 14 x 18 inch rectangle. Spread with soft butter, leaving a ½ inch border unbuttered. Sprinkle with sugar, chopped walnuts, raisins and cinnamon. Starting with long side, roll tightly. Pinch seam to seal. Using a sharp serrated knife, divide roll into 16 pieces. Place, cut side down, in well-buttered 13 x 9 inch baking pan. Cover and let rise about 1 hour, until doubled in size.

Bake at 375°F on middle rack for about 30 minutes. Let stand 5 minutes before inverting pan. Makes 16

11

KALYNA COUNTRY

Kalyna Country runs along the valley of the North Saskatchewan River, accessed by two highways—the Yellowhead (Hwy 16), and Highway 28, which veers northward to Cold Lake. It's a pretty part of Alberta, farm country with lovely old farmsteads and over 100 Eastern Rite churches, many of which can be visited. That distinctive smell in the autumn air comes from the kalyna—the wild cranberries beloved of early cooks, and still prized.

⊚ WAINWRIGHT

$$ **The Honey Pot Eatery and Pub**
823 2nd Avenue   (780) 842-4094
Open Monday–Saturday 11:00 AM–9:30 PM; Sunday brunch 11:00 AM–2:00 PM
V, MC, AE

> Alex and Jeannie Heath have taken over the venerable Honey Pot, a regional favourite since it opened in 1979. The concept has grown, and now includes a pub with the same menu as the dining room.
>
> Alberta beef is their specialty, with tender steaks leading the pack, and there's are also the baby back ribs, pasta dishes and their popular chef's salad. Desserts are locally made, and the Oreo cheesecake and turtle cheesecake are both crowd pleasers. The day we visited, the famous suicide cake wasn't available. Pity; the Food Lovers love cake.

⊚ VERMILION

Vermilion Agricultural Fair   www.town.vermilion.ab.ca
Last weekend in July   (780) 853-4108

Big bench show, and on the grounds, you can eat fresh baked pies contributed by local good cooks. Every night, St. Olga's Church puts on a Ukrainian supper.

$$

Tuscany Grill

5030 49th Avenue   (780) 853-2755

Open Monday–Saturday 11:00 AM–10:00 PM

Sunday 11:00 AM–9:00 PM

V, MC, DEBIT

> Lorene and Jack Achtay are a Lebanese couple running a steak, pizza and pasta place here in mid-Alberta. They do a great steak sandwich and make a landmark Ukrainian pizza—thick crust, bacon, garlic sausage, roasted garlic. Special menus for kids and seniors.

The Orchard Palace

Between Two Hills and St. Paul at Brousseau, off Hwy 36   (780) 657-2275

Open mid-July–September

> There's nothing better than picking apples on a brilliant fall day—the aroma of winey sap, the fall colours, the crisp air. Victor and Elizabeth Krapko's ranch is gradually becoming the first major apple orchard in Alberta. They planted the original saplings in 1997, so it's still a young orchard, with 2000 trees, 1500 of which are apples—63 named varieties at the moment. The rest of the orchard is in pears, plums and pie cherries, with some saskatoons and raspberries. As with all U-Picks, be sure to call first to see if they're picking that day.

◎ VEGREVILLE

Prime Cuts Meat and Deli

5029 50th Street   (780) 632-6149

Open Monday–Friday 9:00 AM–5:00 PM

Saturday 9:00 AM–4:00 PM

DEBIT

> Makers of Vegreville Garlic Sausage, a traditional Ukrainian garlic sausage; kubyburgers garlic sausage patties; ham sausage and beef jerky.

Vegreville Ukrainian Pysanka Festival   www.vegrevillefestival.com

Vegreville Fair Grounds   (780) 632-2777

> Immerse yourself in three days of Ukrainian celebrations on the first weekend in July—food, dance, folk art, beer garden, bread baking demos. You'll find big line-ups for the authentic Ukrainian food—pyrohy, holubtsi, all the kubasa you can eat.

⊚ MUNDARE

In the town made famous by a towering ring of kubasa, Stawnichy's Meat Processing offers tours by arrangement, Tuesday–Thursday. Call (780) 764-3912.

$ **M&M's Kozy Kitchen**

5029 50th Street   (780) 764-2227

Open Tuesday, Wednesday 8:00 AM–6:00 PM

Thursday–Saturday 8:00 AM–7:00 PM

Sunday 10:00 AM–2:00 PM

V, MC, JBL, DEBIT

> People love the Ukrainian plate with cabbage rolls, pyrohy, and Stawnichy's sausage—what else? They make an excellent bowl of borscht. The big breakfast is a big seller: sausage, bacon, ham, homegrown potatoes with skin on (we're talking real home fries) plus three eggs and toast.

Glendon: The Pyrohy Trail Revisted

We love this little burg for its sheer chutzpah. It's a 75-year-old hamlet with a population of 480, and the residents hitched their star to the local hero—not a hockey player or a politician, but a humble boiled dumpling known as the pyrohy, or pyrogy, depending on which cook you talk to. Where, but in feisty little Glendon, would the populace erect a giant fiberglass version of a dumpling, name a park and their main street after it, and sponsor a pyrohy eating contest to take place during (you guessed it) Pyrogyfest, come September.

We also love the 12-table Pyrogy Park Café, where the enterprising restaurateur, Thanh Ngo, late of Vietnam, offers both Chinese pyrogies (meat, onion, sealed in a wonton wrapper, deep-fried, served with plum sauce) and Ukrainian pyrogies (potato dumplings filled with cheddar and potatoes, served with sour cream). If you aren't a pyrogy fan, he'll whip up a batch of poutine, or the Glendon special (a burger) or even the Mixed Grill, Glendon Style. Should you happen to be in Glendon on the second Saturday of August, you'll be smack dab in the middle of Berry Daze, just in time for the pancake breakfast and parade. Roll on, Glendon!

⊚ ASHMONT

Kountry Korner

Hwy 28 at Ashmont turnoff   (780) 726-4079

Open 7:00 AM–9:00 PM

CASH

> Essentially a family-owned and -operated spot, this tiny café does a good, big breakfast called the Boss Hawg Country Morning Feast—three eggs, ham, sausage, bacon, bologna, the country-style beans made from scratch, home fries, three slices of toast and coffee. The Kountry burger involves ham, bacon and a special house sauce. All meals include soup and dessert of the day.

⊚ VILNA

The town of Vilna has embarked on a major facelift. Through the Alberta Mainstreet Program, it has developed a certain movie-set charm. Several false front shops are painted bright colours, and have adopted snappy awnings. On the nearby back roads, check out Kubasa Canyon on County Road 110 E, south of Vilna, and the lovely old Eastern Rite Dickiebush Church, high on the hill. It's a beautiful drive, spring or fall.

Vilna Hotel

5036 50th Street   (780) 636-3524

> You've probably come to see the giant mushrooms swaying gracefully in the park. Everybody else does. There once was a cheerful butter-coloured dining room in the Vilna Hotel—simple, with excellent burgers and home-cut fries. We loved the airy cinnamon buns, yeasty, fresh, with raisins and all that lovely sticky syrup. The pie was among the best we've eaten: fresh apple, excellent pumpkin, or lemon meringue. Now, it's a registry office. A cryin' shame, we say. We're told the kitchen is still open, with the same cook, and you can still eat in the (very smoky) bar, worth a try.

Vilna Foods

Main Street   (780) 636-3573

Open Monday–Saturday 9:00 AM–9:00 PM

Sundays and Holidays 10:00–6:00 PM

V, DEBIT

> If you're provisioning for a picnic, this old-timey general store has all you need, including a small section of deli meats and some fresh produce. We're told that someone bakes fresh bread, "In the back, Monday to Friday."

On the first Saturday in October, the Great White North Pumpkin Fair brings people to this pretty town in droves. We love coming here in pumpkin season, but there are other reasons to linger in Smoky Lake.

The Smoky Lake Inn

4 Wheatland Avenue   (780) 656-3615

Open Monday–Saturday 6:30 AM–9:00 PM

Sunday 7:30 AM–9:00 PM

V, MC, DEBIT

It doesn't look like much from the outside, but this place is blessed with a terrific cook. The rib-sticking breakfasts—eggs, sausages, bacon, scratch pancakes—can come with house-made pyrohy instead of home fries. The cook does the essential Ukrainian platter, the pyrohy and cabbage roll plate and the quarter ring of kubasa side order. There are weekly evening specials. Her pies and pastries are outstanding. "We do saskatoon and rhubarb when it's in season, and during the Fair, everything is pumpkin, even the soup . . ." says the cook.

Brian and Leesa Jones took over the hotel a few years back and are slowly upgrading the property. Fresh brewed coffee in a choice of blends and the excellent selection of teas on offer.

Look for the sunflowers

Linda's Market Garden and Country Kitchen   (780) 656-2401

Hwy 28 Smoky Lake

Linda Christensen has found her niche. When country women began working off the farm, their traditional big gardens became a problem. That's when Linda began growing the gardens they no longer had time for, supplying everything from bedding plants to seasonal produce.

She started with two rows of cucumbers, and most of her cucumber crop was sold fresh. Then, when the same women no longer had time to make their own pickles, she added dills to her list.

Gradually, people began asking for crops she hadn't yet grown, so she expanded: a farmgate stand and 20-acre vegetable garden, plus a country store on Highway 28, near Smoky Lake.

"We grow and sell young potatoes, peas, cucumbers, sweet corn, cabbage, pumpkins, both at the farmgate and at our country store, as well as three farmers' markets," she says breathlessly. "And we operate a 6000-square-foot greenhouse."

Last year she put in a commercial kitchen so she could sell a few value-added products. In season there's ice cream with strawberries, country-themed gifts, and every Friday is pyrohy night.

Baba's Bistro

Junction of Hwy 28 and Hwy 63   (780) 736-3752
Open daily 6:30 AM–10:00 PM
V, MC, DEBIT

> When Peter Lee bought the Rosenbary Mohawk from Rose and Bary Lyle, the café became Baba's Bistro. Nothing fancy, just home-cooked food. They do a roast pork dinner, and there's the Wasketenau Whopper (a biggish burger). If you're a bold eater, you could consider the Great Pyrohy Challenge—not for the weak of heart, you'll need to down 50 pyrohy in 25 minutes. It's free if you can do it, and you get your name on the infamous Baba's Hall of Fame Plaque. If you fail, it'll cost you $24.99. Individual eaters only please, no sharing under the table. Try the excellent nalysnyky—tiny, tender crepes with a dilled cheese filling.

⊚ R E D W A T E R

Redwater River Ranch

Hwy 28, Redwater, watch for signage   ·   (780) 942-2699
Open daily 8:30 AM–9:00 PM

> The Lakusta family has 200 elk and 120 bison, and makes several varieties of sausage. This is a well-run farmgate operation with frozen product.

Coronado Saskatoon Farm

56522 Range Road 231 (east of Hwy 28)
Seasonal, call first

> This U-pick operation offers many different varieties of Saskatoons. Occasionally there are saskatoon pies and juice for sale, and the Coronado sells fruit to several Edmonton restaurants including the Upper Crust (V1 p. 86, 138) and the unheardof (V1 p. 126).

Alpine Farm

54207 Range Road 275, west of St. Albert on Secondary Hwy 633   (780) 963-9291
Seasonal, call first

> A taste of Bavaria on the Prairies. Rainer and Anne Hartl make excellent European-style breads, soups, traditional Bavarian dishes. How about a day of hiking, yodelling, and breaking bread with friends at this lovely Alpine-style country house?

$$ **Mundare Sausage House, Uncle Ed's Restaurant**
11401 50th Street   (780) 471-1010
Open Monday–Saturday, 11:00 AM–6:30 PM
V, MC, DEBIT

> Plate #1 is the most popular combo here: Stawnichy sausage, pyrohy, cheese bun, cheese crepe and cabbage rolls, your choice sweet or sour cabbage. They also make a good bowl of borscht. There's an attached deli, opening a bit earlier at 8:30 AM.

Pyrohy Supper

Holy Cross Ukrainian Catholic Church   (780) 476-2982 for information
9003 153rd Avenue

Father Don Bodnar and about 800 of his friends and parishioners get together every two months or so to eat pyrohy, socialize and support the church and community. The team of pyrohy enthusiasts, led by chief pyrohy wrangler Judy Mydan, spend most of a week preparing for these feasts.

For openers, the team peels about 400 pounds of potatoes by hand ("We need the potato water," says Judy). They hand-roll the dough, cut it, fill it with cheddar and seasoned potato, parboil it, chill and freeze the finished dumplings.

"We made 1000 dozen pyrohys this time," says Judy. "It's like doing three weddings. The cheddar always goes first."

The line-up was already out the door when we got there just before 5:00 PM. The buffet stretched across the hall—pyrohy, fried onions, mushrooms in cream with garlic and dill, lazy cabbage roll casserole, the definitive garlic sausage from Widynowski's Sausage in Beverly. Then there was the giant Caesar salad, the buns and the batter-fried codfish.

Here's your chance to sit down over traditional Ukrainian food with friendly people of distant Italian, Chinese and other ancestry. These suppers are true community builders. You don't have to be Ukrainian to enjoy this feast, and at $10 a head at deadline, it's a cheap date. Beer and wine are available. Father Don won't let you out the door without buying a copy of the official parish cookbook, well worth the price.

PHOTO COURTESY JUDY SCHULTZ

FROM VOLUME ONE WE STILL LIKE

The Alberta Hotel, Vegreville (780) 632-3528 (p. 146); the Josephsburg Fried Chicken Supper (780) 998-9450 (p. 150); the Old Fashioned Bread Bakery, Smoky Lake (780) 656-3780 (p. 149); Great White North Pumpkin Fair, Smoky Lake (780) 656-3674 (p. 148); Maple Tree Grill, Waskatenau (780) 358-2882 (p. 147); Maria's Place, Edmonton (780) 474-4059 (p. 144); St. Basil's Edmonton (780) 434-4288 (p. 142).

Kalyna Country Spring Borsch

6 small beets with tops
1 large onion, chopped
1 large carrot, diced
1 medium potato, diced
1 stalk celery, diced
4 cups (1 L) shredded green cabbage
6 cups (1.5 L) chicken or beef stock
2 cups (500 mL) water
4 cups (1 L) canned tomatoes with juice
½ lemon
1 tablespoon (15 mL) sugar
¼ cup fresh dillweed, chopped
salt, pepper
sour cream

Wash beets. Clip tops and wash, discarding any that aren't in good shape. Chop beet tops and reserve. Scrub beets well, but do not peel. Slice into thin strips. Place all vegetables except beet tops and tomatoes in a large soup pot with meat stock and water. Simmer until vegetables are tender. Add tomatoes, lemon juice and skin of ½ lemon, and sugar. Simmer 15 minutes. Remove lemon skin. Add reserved beet tops and dillweed. Cook 5 minutes. Taste, and correct seasoning with salt and pepper. Serve hot, topped with a spoonful of sour cream.

Serves 10 to 12

PRODUCERS

Patty Milligan AKA Lola Canola

Bees are one of the insect world's most intriguing creatures. Ask any beekeeper. Patty Milligan's fascination with bees led her to start a small apiary where she produces seasonal, varietal and infused honey. "For every flower there's a honey," says the woman farmers' markets know as Lola Canola. "Some of us have been building on that."

Varietal honeys are always a challenge because of the short flowering season, so she gets a jump on it with her main varietal—willow honey. "Willow produces the first flowers of spring, pussy willows. Varietals take extra management and organization. The bees actually need this early nectar to get them over the long winter, so I might only get 100 pounds of willow honey."

It's a drop in the barrel when you consider the thousands of tonnes of honey produced in an Alberta summer, but for Patty, it's worth the trouble.

"I want to try raspberry honey and borage honey. I also make some infused honeys—rose, lavender, mint."

She looks for unique patches of wildflowers—fireweed, dandelion, sweet clover. "I'm starting to move my bees on special wagons, so they can take advantage of the short blossom season."

Watch for her at the Edmonton City Market, Sherwood Park and Beverley Towne. Chef Brad Lazarenko of Culina in Edmonton uses her willow honey as a glaze for lamb chops. Lola Canola Kid's Club newsletter is available four times per year. Write to: Box 654 Bon Accord TOA OKO.

Brassica Mustard

606 23rd Avenue NE   (403) 277-3301

Calgary

Alberta produces most of the mustard seed used for mustard making all over the world. But until now, very little of this seed stayed here. Karen Davis and chef Desmond Johnson have developed a line of all-Alberta gourmet mustards available at food shops such as at Janice Beaton Fine Cheese in Calgary. ***

Brightbank Finnsheep

Spruce Grove   (780) 963-0416

Ralph and Kathy Playdon raise Finnsheep on their Spruce Grove farm. The lambs are pastured, and their feed is supplemented with grain. Finnsheep lamb is lean and sweet.

Note: Ralph is also known as the shepherd of Fort Saskatchewan's celebrity flock of 50 ewes, where they've become a major tourist attraction in the town.

Cakadu Heritage Lamb   cakadu@telusplanet.net

Linda Jabs   (403) 728-2398

The Cakadu lamb, a Caribbean hair sheep, produces lean, tasty meat with little lanolin and no tallowy taste, so you can even eat it cold. They take ten months to mature at their own free-range pace. "We can't get a lamb to market within the usual (commercial) 120 days, and we don't want to try," says Linda. The flock is shepherded by a pair of Tuscan herding dogs, Jude and Dog, "And we haven't lost a sheep." The sheep have generous pasture on the Jabs' 160 acres west of Innisfail in central Alberta. Lambs cruise around, munching grass, ignoring their winter shelter because, "they like to see sky."

Chickadee Farm

Flatbush

Organic herbal teas and a variety of culinary and healing herbs are all grown and harvested in a pristine environment. Available through health food stores such as Planet Organic.

De la Terre Farms

Athabasca   (780) 675-3716

Tom Kraweic and Janice Baker raise pastured pork and Katahdin lamb on their farm near Athabasca. These hogs are almost entirely fed on alfalfa pasture, with a supplement of beet pulp, flax meal and canola meal added when the pasture season is over. The livestock is grazed on fresh pasture daily, and trained to come to a bell. "We believe this is a healthy way to raise them," says Tom. "They experience no stress, and that leads to healthy livestock."

An order of a side of pork typically includes chops, steak, shoulder roast, ribs, ground pork, sliced bacon, a picnic roast, cutlets, ham and breakfast sausage. All meat is government inspected, cryovaced and freezer-ready.

Also available through De la Terre: Katahdin lamb, La Bon Petite Beef (Dexter-Piedmontese), free-range turkeys, free-range eggs. The meat is available direct, and monthly deliveries can be arranged.

Double R Game Farm

Onoway   (780) 967-3537

> Farmgate only. Double R sells elk meat, elk jerky, garlic sausage, pepperoni and a variety of frozen elk products including steaks.

Driview Farms

Fort Macleod   (403) 553-2178

> Gerrit and Janet Van Hierden have raised lamb on their farm near Fort Macleod for over 25 years. This is beautiful meat, home grown, grain fed. Rouge restaurant in Calgary serves Driview lamb. You can purchase from the family at the Millarville Market, and in Calgary at the Northland's Market, or call them. They also make a seasoning mix, mint sauce and mint jelly—just the thing with their lamb.

Edelweiss Foods

St. Albert   (780) 699-7978

> Several Edmonton and area restaurants have discovered Luke Gorbahn's well-made camembert and brie-style cheeses. They're available at Sobey's in St. Albert.

Edgar Farms   www.edgarfarms.com

10 km west of Innisfail

Open daily, May through September

> Doug and Elna Edgar have been raising green asparagus on their farm near Innisfail since 1986. During its short season, early May through June, they sell it by the bunch in their farmgate shop. Drive into the yard; the shop is at the front of the barn, and there's an honesty box so you can pay for your purchases if they aren't there.
>
> In asparagus season, it takes a crew of seven pickers to harvest the 27 kilo-metres of asparagus rows in the Edgar's 6.8 hectare patch. Spears are picked daily. If they're allowed to get too tall, they'll open into a fern—lovely to look at, but not much good with hollandaise.
>
> "We stop picking early enough so the plants can send up fern, which supplies valuable nutrients to the crowns," says Elna.
>
> After asparagus season they sell their peas and beans, Beck Farm carrots, C&J tomatoes, strawberries from The Jungle, and other produce. The Edgars also have cattle, plus 25 acres of market garden peas, and are part of the five-family Innisfail Growers Co-Op.
>
> Their asparagus is available at the Old Strathcona Market, Innisfail Market, Red Deer, Lacombe, and three Calgary markets—Northland's, Hillhurst and Currie Barracks.

Doug and Elna Edgar

COURTESY OF DOUG AND ELNA EDGAR

Asparagus Salad with Grape Tomatoes

1 pound (500 g) medium asparagus, trimmed
1 tablespoon (15 mL) soy sauce
1 tablespoon (15 mL) sesame oil
2 teaspoons (10 mL) red wine vinegar
2 teaspoons (10 mL) sugar
1 pint box currant tomatoes, cleaned

Slice asparagus on the diagonal into 2-inch lengths. Reserve the tips separately. Mix all other ingredients and heat together until sugar is dissolved. Bring a pot of water to a boil. Drop in asparagus stem cuts and cook 1 minute. Add tips and cook 30 seconds more, until they turn bright green. Drain and immediately refresh under cold water. Put in a bowl with currant tomatoes and drizzle with the soy mixture. Toss and serve.

Serves 6

Dirt Willy Farm
Ardrossan

www.dirtwilly.com
(780) 922-6080

If you think a guy named Dirt Willy probably raises earthworms, you're right. "It's true, I raise red wigglers for the Grade 4 Alberta curriculum." But Rick Wood-Samman, AKA Dirt Willy, is also in the luxury game bird business, acting as hatcher, breeder and processor at his place in Ardrossan, along the west boundary of Elk Island Park.

"We're a federally registered hatchery, specializing in three species of wild turkeys—Merriam, Eastern and Rio Grande—and three species of pheasants: coloured jumbo ringnecks, bred for size and colour; whites, developed with no dark pinfeathers for the restaurant trade; and the smaller Chinese ringneck."

Oddly enough, wild turkeys roost in trees, and they do love to fly. "We've lost one that way," he says. "I opened the door to the pen, and she took off and just kept going."

Rick's wild birds, including his chukar partridges, are sold to restaurants all over Alberta:

"Chukars are very lean. The trick with these birds is to never, ever overcook them. When the juice runs clear, they're done."

He gives away a small cookbook with every bird he sells. "It's guidance for first-timers. If they don't know how to cook the birds they might end up with dry meat." Dirt Willy's is a farmgate business, afternoons only. "Just call ahead," he says. "It's a real pretty drive."

Dirt Willy's Deep-Fried Wild Turkey

"Buy the special gas base from Superstore," he says, "or I can sell you one." It's like a big bunsen burner, with an aluminum pot and a submersible basket. Marinate the bird if you wish, but pat it dry before you put it in the oil. Pour about 12 litres of canola oil into your pot. It has to cover the bird completely. Set it up outside—never in your house.

Bring the oil to 350°F. Carefully immerse the bird in the basket. Cook it 3 minutes per pound, plus an additional 5 minutes. The hot oil will seal the meat. You can reuse it three times; freezing after each use.

Farmers' Market Vegetables in Dill Cream

This is an old Prairie recipe for creamed new vegetables. All of them—baby potatoes, young carrots, peas and dill—can be purchased at optimum freshness at a farmers market.

1 lb (500 g) new potatoes
8 oz (250 g) bunch new carrots
8 oz bunch (250 g) green or yellow beans
1 cup (250 g) shelled peas
1 tablespoon (15 mL) butter
1 tablespoon (15 mL) cornstarch
1 cup (250 mL) 2 per cent milk
4 oz. light cream cheese, cubed, room temperature
¼ cup (50 mL) chopped fresh dillweed
salt and freshly ground pepper

Bring a large pot of water to a boil. Add salt and potatoes. Boil about 5 minutes, and add carrots. Continue cooking until carrots are barely tender. Break beans into thirds and add to boiling vegetables. As soon as they change colour, add peas. Cook another 3 minutes. Drain, reserving ½ cup of cooking liquid. Return liquid to the pot, with 1 tablespoon butter. Turn heat to low.

Dissolve cornstarch in cold milk. Pour into vegetable pot and turn heat up to medium. Add cubed cream cheese. Cook, stirring gently, until sauce is thick and creamy. Add chopped dillweed, salt and pepper, and serve. Serves 4 to 6

Fairwinds Farm
Fort Macleod   (403) 553-0127
Ben and Anita Oudshoorn

"This is not what we planned," says Anita wryly. "We went on a tour to Natrica Dairy and started to build up a herd to supply them with milk. We enjoy the farming. We never thought we'd be in the yogurt business."

When Natrica closed, the Oudshoorns were left with a lovely herd of Alpines and Nubians in need of regular milking. The business started slowly, with milk for local stores and Marra's in Canmore. Now they make eight different flavours of yogurt (plain is still the biggest seller) and are developing a chevre. "It's in the family testing stages," says Anita.

Ah, the life of the lonely goat herder. "Mondays are marathon days," says Ben. "We milk, pack, load, put everything together for our northern run."

You can find Fairwinds milk and yogurt (and soon their soft cheese) at Marra's in Canmore; in Calgary at Community, Sunterra and Amaranth; in Edmonton at Save-on-Foods, Planet Organic, Sunterra, Organic Roots and Big Fresh; in Lethbridge at Save-On, Or-Kids Organic Market; in Red Deer at Save-On and IGA; and in assorted Co-ops in smaller centres.

First Nature Farm
Goodfare (780) 356-2239

Jerry Kitt raises certified organic chicken, bison, beef and pastured Landrace-Yorkshire pork on a farm near the BC border. His products are available at the Old Strathcona Market in Edmonton. Fresh turkeys are available for Thanksgiving and Christmas.

Greens, Eggs and Ham Family Farm
Leduc (780) 986-8680

Mary Ellen and Andreas Grueneberg grow heirloom, odd and unusual vegetables—rosara, bintje, Russian purple, and almondine potatoes; cylinder, golden, chiogga and red beets; dill, borage, cinnamon basil; green, yellow, fava and scarlet runner beans; shelling peas, edible flowers, kohlrabi, several different cucumbers, plus orach (maroon spinach) and corn. They also raise several kinds of fowl, chicken, turkey, ducks and duck eggs.

Hillman's Greenhouse
(780) 582-2240

Claire and Ken Hillman have a large market garden near Forestburg, where Claire is known as the tomato lady. We love field tomatoes for their great flavour and unique acid balance.

Iowalta Gardens
(403) 782-1543

Joan Tancock grows fresh herbs, often working with Linda Boang of Sunridge Greenhouses. You'll find the herbs on menus around Edmonton and at farmers markets.

Kickin' Ash Buffalo
54416 Range Road 274, Calahoo (780) 460-1700

Their grandfather homesteaded this land in the early 1900s. Paul and Perry Kolesar sell farm direct and at the Stony Plain Market every Saturday. The meat is grain finished 120 days minimum on oats or barley, then aged 21 days.

Sage Kitchen

Turner Valley

www.sagekitchen.com
(403) 933-4882, 1 888 497-9929

When Pam Vipond moved her operation from Golden to Invermere. she started selling edible flower jellies at the Millarville Farmers' Market. There, she discovered that most of the bedding plant folks had empty greenhouses by mid-June. Now, they're filled with her edible flowers, providing a second season of income for the growers. The growers supply good soil supplemented with compost, and she rotates flowers regularly. The ladybugs take care of the insects, boiling water looks after the ants, cats hunt down the mice and the dogs scare away the deer who love to nibble on the flowers.

Pam makes a variety of jellies and packages what she calls edible confetti (petals) in both a sweet and savoury mix. The sweet contains calendula, clove pinks, roses and pansies for baking. The savoury has chive blossoms, marigolds and squash blossoms, ideal to flavour a salad dressing. Sage Kitchen is available at Sunterra and Olive Me in Edmonton, and Sunterra and Red Tree Kitchen in Calgary. Or go see Pam at the Millarville Farmers' Market.

Ladybug Organic Produce

Markerville

(403) 728-0700

Janette Jones grows certified organic potatoes, strawberries, garlic and parsnips. You'll find her veggies at farmers' markets and in a few chefs' kitchens.

Lalany's International Meats Inc.

www.lalanys.com

(780) 988-6373

The Lalany family have a bison ranch west of Edmonton and they've concentrated on value added products. You can find their bison entrées in teriyaki, Malaysian curry and the award winning Spice Island. New products are the Malaysian curry sauce and a low-fat Mediterranean bison meat sauce with five different vegetables. Look for these products at Save-On-Foods and other retailers. Their plans for expansion were hit hard by the drought and BSE related issues, yet they have joined other small Alberta food processors to find ways to work together and promote their products as the Specialty Foods Network.

Norberry Orchards

Red Deer

(403) 773-2489

Open Monday–Friday 8:00 AM–4:30 PM

The Deliadais family, with several other growers under the Norberry Orchards banner tend 200 acres of heritage berries—saskatoons, blackcurrants and wild black cherries—all indigenous to this part of the country. The berries grow in coulees, protected from the wind, all across the central prairies. You can pick saskatoons during the week. They process purées, syrups, juices and pie fillings from these intensely flavoured, nutritious berries under the brand PNP (Prairie Natural Processing). Call for information on the dates for the annual open house Alberta Fruit festival.

Doug and Evelyn Visser, Riverbend Gardens

During the summer season, Doug and Evelyn Visser and their family are preoccupied with vegetables: cabbage, cauliflower, broccoli, field cucumbers, potatoes, carrots, corn, peas and beans. "The only things we don't grow are greenhouse crops," says Doug, who has been selling garden produce at farmers' markets since 1981.

The Vissers started with one market, and now operate stalls in six local markets every week during the season—Sherwood Park Festival Place, the 104 Street City Market, the Beverley Towne, the Old Strathcona, the Fort Saskatchewan and the St. Albert markets.

"Our place is probably a little too far out of town for a farmgate store," he says, reflecting on the logistics of running a six-location business, constantly chauffering cabbages and tomatoes to keep supplies topped up.

"We learned from others—people like Dietrich and Elizabeth Kuhlmann, and Lois Hole and her family, back when the Holes were still in this business." The Visser stalls are always busy, surrounded two-deep by a queue of shoppers who know these vegetables are only a few hours out of the ground or off the vine.

O Foods
Didsbury

Dando1@telus.net
(403) 829-6405

Diana and Derek Daunheimer farm just north of Didsbury. They grow cool climate vegetables, according to Diana "things that do well in the field here." This includes greens, radishes, beans, peas, root vegetables. They forage for wild roses, spruce tips and other wild things for several restaurant customers, including Infuse Catering and River Café in Calgary and the Banfshire Club in Banff. Their farm is an example of the long, careful process that leads to becoming a certified organic farm. Their land has been free of any external chemical regime since 1962. It's currently called transitional, and will be certified organic in 2005. Expect the U-pick and farm stand to be open most Saturdays come summer, but it's always a good idea to call first.

Paradise Hill Farm
Nanton

hillfarm@telusplanet.net
(403) 646-3276

Schools often tour this greenhouse and cattle operation where you can purchase pesticide-free cucumbers, basil, strawberries and vine ripened tomatoes at the farm store, as well as their own beef and lamb.

Peace Gourmet Honey—Jean's Bees

Hines Creek   (780) 494-2875

Jean Coppens d'Eeckenbrugge

Last year, Jean lost 80 per cent of his bees to a parasite, dropping from 100 producing hives to 20. He was able to build up to 50 hives by the end of the summer by collecting swarms—the cloud of bees that sometimes spontaneously take flight. This is not a job for the faint of heart.

Jean puts his hives by fields of white clover, fireweed and alfalfa. He stays away from canola, not liking the flavour and its tendency to cystallize in the hive, making it hard for the bees to overwinter. He also doesn't take off the early spring willow honey, believing that he's too far north. "My bees overwinter in a willow grove," he says. "They need the energy from the pussywillows, then dandelion, then chokecherries." Peace Gourmet Honey is available directly from Jean if you're in the area. His varietal honeys are worth the trip.

Pine Terra Farm

Onoway   (780) 967-3012, 1-800-674-2333

The Phillips family has owned and operated this farm since 1937, and has never used pesticides, fertilizers or herbicides on their land. The product is certified organic grass fed Alberta Angus beef. Buy this beef at the St. Albert Farmers' Market, or call and order direct.

Pepperheads of Canada

Turner Valley   www.pepperheadscanada.com

         (403) 680-7669

D'arcy McCrea

They call themselves the tasteful little company from Turner Valley. There are several excellent condiments: the original hot sauce, Dark Secrets BBQ sauce, Piri Piri wing sauce (great on a tuna sandwich). The condiments are widely available across Alberta, Back Country Butcher in Cowley, Marras in Canmore, Thymes Two in Edson and Sunterra, and Barbecue County in Edmonton. Be sure to check out the award-winning website. It's fun and informative.

Poplar Bluff Farm

Strathmore   (403) 934-5400

Rosemary Wotske-Giberson is known for her multiple varieties of potatoes, including four different fingerlings, some of which date back to the 1800s. Then there's adora, a new variety with 30 per cent fewer carbs than a traditional russet potato. "There are some wonderful new yellow potatoes," says Rosemary, "Yellow as a phone book, with fabulous flavour."

Poplar Bluff has been experimenting with ways to store potatoes without using sprout inhibitors. One promising method is fogging the cold room with essential oils of mint, caraway or dill. This practice dates back to the Incas, who were known to bury their spuds with herb leaves. Good restaurants snap up these potatoes—Il Sogno, River Café, the Hyatt, Divino. Look for them at Community Natural Foods, Amaranth, Sunnyside Market and Planet Organic, all in Calgary.

Red Willow Gardens

Beaverlodge (780) 354-8211

Eric and Carmen Deschipper grow carrots, cucumbers, potatoes, fresh greens and other vegetables on their farm down by the river, just south of Beaverlodge. You can buy their produce on site, or look for them at local farmers' markets. There is a tea shop with a large deck, homemade soups, sandwiches and carrot cake made with their own carrots. Call for tea shop hours, as they vary with the picking schedule. Open during the summer.

The Prairie Emporium Arrow Gardens

Strathmore

www.albertafruit.com

(403) 934-5796

East of Strathmore on north side of Hwy 1

Natural beef, bedding plants and pastured poultry, local crafts, seasonal produce.

Spruce Park Ranch

51432 RR 273, Spruce Grove (780) 963-5235

The Trautman family raise the Katahdin variety of lamb on their ranch west of Edmonton. It's a hair sheep—no wool, and they looks more like goats. The meat is lean and sweet tasting, and is prized by local chefs. It's available through Stony Plain Country Market and by private sale. We've also enjoyed their excellent chickens at the Upper Crust Café in Edmonton.

Sunridge Greenhouses

RR 1, Lacombe (403) 782-5031

The cucumbers, red and green peppers and other vegetables grown by Linda Boang and family find their way onto menus at Culina and the Hotel Macdonald. You can find these impeccable vegetables at the New City Market in Edmonton.

Thompson Valley Farms

Edmonton

www.thompsonvalley.com

(780) 435-2393

Lance Thompson is on a mission to tell the world about hemp and its tasty, healthy properties. You can find Lance at the Strathcona Market in Edmonton or the Currie Barracks Market in Calgary. Do stop by his stand—he's entertaining, and you'll walk away with some delicious cold-pressed oil or nutty-tasting hemp seeds to sprinkle on your cereal or salad. You'll find their products on several restaurant menus including Culina. They have recently developed a line of body care products with hemp oil as the base.

True Taste Piedmontese Beef

cmvnstry@telusplanet.net

RR 2 Clive

(403) 784-3519

Marcella Van Stryland

Piedmontese is a lean, double-muscled breed with what cattle breeders refer to as a "tender gene." Originally from northern Italy, they were introduced to Canada several decades ago. Van Stryland's feeding program includes grass, forage, and 120 day grain-finishing, all on the ranch, rather than a feedlot. Freezer packs are available at their on-farm store, Second to None Meats in Calgary, Red Deer and Lacombe farmers markets.

Vital Green Organic Milk

Picture Butte

(403) 634-1197

Joe and Carolyn Manns

It's almost unheard-of to drink milk from cows that ate grass all summer—something out of a storybook. Yet one couple is doing just that with their certified organic milk, Vital Green.

Joe Manns had worked in a dairy for several years and saw the opportunity to start a dairy of his own a few years ago. Cattle prices were low, and because they wanted to produce organic milk, they could lease quota directly from the Dairy Board. The Manns started small with 22 cows.

"The cows eat grass all summer, producing a milk that's high in CLA (conjugate linoleic acid—the good stuff). In the winter we feed them our own hay." They started with whole milk but now produce skim, 1 and 2 per cent plus a full-fat chocolate milk. The little bit of ultra rich cream is sold at Sunworks. "We just made some buttermilk, and I'm testing cottage cheese," he says.

Vital Green milk is available in Edmonton at Organic Roots and Planet Organic, in Calgary at Community Natural Foods, Planet Organic, Amaranth, Farm Fresh Deliveries, Currie Barracks Farmers Market, and in Lethbridge at the Harvest Haven Farm store.

Wolfe Honey Co.

Guy

(780) 925-2463

Gilbert and Sharon Wolfe operate the family honey company in an expanded processing facility in the hamlet of Guy. They ship their delicate clover honey all over the world, and the renowned Ace Bakery in Toronto uses their organic honey. In the winter the queens take a vacation, spending the winter in the balmy weather of the Fraser Valley. This is how they're able to build hives and start honey production earlier in the season. Call first before visiting.

ALL-ALBERTA FARMERS' MARKET LISTING

These are some of our favourite Farmers' Markets. Times, dates and even locations are subject to change, so we've included phone numbers.

For complete listings of market gardens and U-picks throughout the province go to www.albertafarmfresh.ca or call 1-800-661-2642.

CALGARY

Calgary Farmers Market Currie Barracks
Hangar #6, 4421 Quesnay Drive SW
Tel: (403) 299-4400
Open year-round 10:00 AM–3 PM
see profile page 39.

Calgary Hillhurst/Sunnyside
1320 5th Avenue, NW (Hillhurst/Sunnyside Community Centre)
Tel: (403) 283-0554
Open June–October 3 Wednesday 3:30 PM–8:00 PM, special Thanksgiving market

CAMROSE
4702 50th Avenue (Elks Hall)
Tel: (780) 672-8930
Open year-round Saturday 8:00 AM–12:00 PM, special Christmas markets in December

DEVON
Community Centre on Haven Avenue
Tel: (780) 987-4046
Open June–October Thursday 2:00 PM–6:00 PM, special Christmas market in November

EDMONTON

Edmonton Callingwood
6655 178th Street (the Marketplace at Callingwood)
Tel: (780) 487-8649
Open May–October 31 Sunday and Wednesday

Edmonton City
104th Street north of 102nd Avenue
Tel: (780) 424-9001
Open Saturday 10:00 AM–3:00 PM, special markets during bedding plant season

Edmonton Old Strathcona
103rd Street and 83rd Avenue (Old Bus Barn)
Tel: (780) 439-1844
Open year-round Saturday 8:00 AM–3:00 PM, special markets throughout the year

LETHBRIDGE
Lethbridge Exhibition
3401 Parkside Drive S (Whoop-up Pavilion)
Tel: (403) 328-4491
Open June–October 31 Saturday 8:00 AM–12:30 PM, special market during Fair Week
(July) in Pioneer Park

MILLARVILLE
Millarville Fairground
Tel: (403) 931-2404
Open June 16–October 6 Saturday 8:30 AM–12:00 PM

RED DEER
43rd Street and 48th Avenue
Tel: (403) 346-6443 / (403) 350-5670
Open mid-May–early October Saturday 8:00 AM–12:30 PM

ST. ALBERT
Grandin Park Plaza (spring and fall location)
St. Anne's and St. Thomas (downtown location for summer) in front of Arden Theatre.
Tel: (780) 458-2833
Open April 1–June 24 Saturday 10:00 AM–3:00 PM, moves to downtown July 1 and moves back to Plaza from October to mid-December

SHERWOOD PARK
Festival Way Parking Lot
Tel: (780) 464-3354
Open May–September 30 Wednesday 5:00 PM–8:30 PM, special market on Canada Day, July 1

VEGREVILLE
5002 55th Avenue (Elks Hall)
Tel: (780) 632-7482
Open March–December 31 Friday 7:30 a.m–12:00 PM, special markets for Father's Day, Thanksgiving, Christmas

VERMILION
5018 49th Avenue (Elks Hall)
Tel: (780) 853-4669
Open February–December Tuesday 10:00 AM–1:00 PM, special Christmas markets through December

WETASKIWIN
Wetaskiwin Mall
Tel: (780) 352-3157
Open January 5–June 28 Wednesday 11:00 AM–4:00 PM

Spring Creek Ranch Premium Natural Beef

Vegreville   www.springcreekranch.com

Spring Creek Ranch Natural Beef is a federally audited program drawing cattle from over 100 ranches. This value chain has standards and processes that sets their product apart from conventional beef. Cattle for Spring Creek Ranch natural beef are segregated and fed a special diet. Should an animal become ill and require antibiotics, it will be removed from the natural beef program and placed in the conventional stream after it recovers.

"Natural beef is about 30 per cent more expensive to produce," says Bern Kotelko, of Highland Feeders near Vegreville. They supply Whole Foods Markets in Vancouver, Toronto and the us, Fairmont Hotels in Canada, and the Westin, Edmonton, with this premium natural beef.

The Kotelko operation is unique in its emphasis on research and environmental stewardship, and Highland Feeders has received many awards for their environmental stewardship. "Due to our recognition, the Alberta Research Council approached us to work with them on a pilot project to convert methane into electricity," says Bern. The test plant was completed in the summer of 2004. Eventually, it could provide power for the ranch and light up a town the size of Vegreville, about 5000 homes. "It's a completely sustainable system," he says. "No waste to haul away, no methane in the air. We'd love to see these in place around the world." Next up is a vertically integrated operation. "We're looking into a project with Sunterra to build and operate a processing plant that is up to the European standard," says Bern. "They want our natural Alberta beef in Europe."

Diamond Willow Range

Twin Butte

To arrange a ranch visit, call Larry Frith (403) 627-2065

There's only one kind of music to be playing when you're travelling the eastern slopes—cowboy music. As we drive through the rolling hills, we listen to local boy

Corb Lund speak of the people who make a life in this gloriously empty landscape.

Certified organic beef producers Diamond Willow Range is a group of seven ranches: Stillridge, Freeman, Salix, Mt. Sentinel, MX, Frith and Ketaorati. These evocative names tell the story of ranching on the eastern slopes.

Diamond Willow came out of a research project by the University of Calgary environmental design department. Were the ranches compatible with wildlife, and were people willing to pay for environmental stewardship at the grocery store?

Yes, on both counts. All seven ranches committed to raising beef in a sustainable manner. Only about 60 per cent of the land is taken up by cattle; the rest is left to wildlife. On average the ratio is about 1 head per 30 acres of land. Diamond Willow believes this low ratio is necessary to ensure the survival of this unique and fragile ecosystem.

Their commitment to long-term sustainable land ownership led to the development of the Southern Alberta Land Trust (SALTS). The cattle are cross-bred, a composite that works for Diamond Willow's A or AA grade, with the leanness characteristic of range-raised animals. All are raised in the balanced ecosystem and low stress environment of the 45,000 or so acres of Eastern slopes controlled by the Diamond Willow Ranches.

Liana Robbericht, executive chef, Calgary Petroleum Club

The Calgary Petroleum is a food and beverage club with an active membership, competing in a city of top-notch restaurants. As their executive chef, Liana Robbericht has 40 staff preparing three meals a day, along with banquets, cocktail parties and other special events. There are three separate kitchens plus prep areas and a full pastry setup.

"Our menus are aggressively Albertan," she says. "At minimum, 70 per cent of ingredients. We contract with several farmers and ranchers—Poplar Bluff for potatoes, Sunworks for chicken. All our mustard is from Brassica, right here

in Calgary. We have a lot of flexibility because we make everything in house— charcuterie, soup, stocks, sauces, breads, pastry. We smoke our salmon here.

"We try to be as seasonal as possible, but people will want strawberries in January. In the late summer, there's lots of great local fruit. We juice it, freeze it, make preserves."

Liana is a self-described food geek. "My mother says that as a toddler, I'd climb up on a stool and want to make dinner. I went through a soufflé stage. I love the simplicity of Asian flavours. I get obsessed with a flavour—lately, it's all about cardamom."

Mentorship has played an important role in Liana's professional life. Yoshi Chubachi, executive chef at the Rimrock Hotel in Banff, was Liana's professional mentor for eleven years. "His influence, and my gratitude, are immeasurable," she says. "I try to do the same in my kitchen. It's part of my value system, to help everybody reach their potential."

Liana sits on the advisory council at SAIT as well as the apprenticeship committee. Her kitchen is a teaching kitchen. "Create the learning envelope," she says. "Move people around so they gain broad experience. If they don't have their red seal, we give them one year's grace, then we expect them to commit to it."

Sal Howell
River Café

Sal's roots in the Calgary scene run deep. She was part of the original team that developed the Mescalero concept, the first Divino, the summer-only River Café, and the extraordinary Teatro. Those were heady days, the beginnings of Calgary's restaurant boom.

Sal's background in fine arts and design was fortuitous. "I was Witold Twardowski's design assistant, then became more involved in all aspects of the business," she says.

"River Café started as a romantic notion of a fishing camp on the Bow River. Our inspiration came from the outdoors. We wanted to serve fish that swam in the river, grains that grew on the plains, fruit that grew in the trees."

River Café's chef Scott Pohorelic works closely with local growers and producers, sourcing much of their food from within a few hours of Calgary. Their commitment to regional cuisine extends to growing their own vegetables at Highwood Crossing Farm, where restaurant staff helps tend the gardens, reveling in the bounty of harvest.

This year Sal returns to River Café on a full time basis. Her business partner, Dario Berloni will assume control at Teatro. "I'm really excited about that. Being involved with both Teatro and River kept me from being hands on," she says. Expect some changes in the

Chef Scott Pohorelic, Sal Howell and Kristi Peters of River Café

wine list. Sal, a certified sommelier, says; "We're not so concerned with trophy wines anymore. I want to move toward something more alive, not just a list of names," she says. "More poetry."

Carol's Cherry Clafouti

Edmonton pastry chef Carol Corneau uses Evans cherries for her cobblers, crisps and other delicious desserts. Note: We prefer this made with fresh cherries—the frozen fruit was too juicy for the batter.

3 cups (750 mL) fresh sour cherries, pitted
¼ cup (50 mL) sugar
¾ cup (175 mL) whole milk
3 eggs
1 tbsp (15 mL) amaretto or other almond liqueur
2 tbsp (30 mL) melted butter
¾ cup (175 mL) flour
¼ cup (50 mL) sugar (second addition)
½ tsp (2 mL) baking powder
¼ tsp (1 mL) salt

Topping:
½ tsp (2 mL) cinnamon
¼ cup (50 mL) sugar

Distribute cherries in a buttered, 10-inch (25 cm) glass pie plate. Sprinkle first addition of sugar over them. Beat together milk, eggs, amaretto and melted butter. Add flour, sugar, baking powder and salt, and beat to a smooth batter. Pour over cherries. Bake at 375°F (190°C) until golden brown and set in the middle. Will puff slightly. Sprinkle with cinnamon and sugar. Let cool in pan 15 minutes before cutting into wedges. Serve warm, with a spoon of whipped cream if you wish to gild the lily.

Evans Cherries

Thanks to the perseverance of several people, including a Devon-area gardener named Ieuan Evans, Albertans now have their own pie cherry, juicy, red, tart-sweet, and big enough to bother pitting.

Evans, a Welsh-born plant-disease specialist, was still working for Alberta Agriculture when he discovered the rogue cherry tree growing in an orchard near Edmonton. The original seedling apparently arrived in Alberta with pioneers from Minnesota, and had been planted near Horse Hill early in the last century. Thus, the Horse Hill cherry, now known as the Evans cherry.

Considered hardy to Zone 2, it is incredibly prolific, producing up to 400 pounds of fruit from a single tree. When a local chef brought the Food Lovers a pail of Evans cherries this year, we made terrific pie, a cherry cobbler, and the best cherry jam we've ever tasted.

Paul Hamer, who owns the Saskatoon Farm at Okotoks, maintains a cherry orchard devoted entirely to Evans. Five more prairie-hardy cherries, as yet unnamed, are also being successfully grown in his orchard.

"Since 1996, we've sold about 30,000 Evans trees per year," Hamer says. "They're hardy—if you know how to grow cherries. Don't over-fertilize or over-water. They need to dry out and harden off in September. Benign neglect is the way to go." Evans cherries and other sour cherries are still pretty much a grow-your-own project, but the fruit has begun showing up at farmers' markets on a now-and-then basis. Watch for them in mid-August.

Arlie's Marketing

arlies@telusplanet.net / (403) 272-2882

Arlie McFadden sells Canadian Rocky Mountain Ranch bison, elk and deer, Galloway Beef from the Folier Farm in Strome, and Winter's Turkey to chefs and independent markets. After 16 years working for a food broker, Arlie went out on her own. "It wasn't by design that I sell only protein. It just worked out that way," she says.

Arlie is known for her marketing skills. In order to introduce bison and elk to the Vancouver market she hired a yacht and took several key Vancouver chefs on a tour up the coast. "We cooked and served tapas of bison and elk. Chefs are so busy, and they love to chat with each other to keep current. We got them together in a collegial environment."

PHOTO COURTESY LORI MENSHIK

Full Course Strategies
(780) 413-9266

Lori Menshik's Full Course Strategies is a one-woman company, but she never feels like she's in business alone. Her business is built on creating partnerships for sustainable agriculture. No matter what the product—baby potatoes, designer cuts of pork, elk steak—there's a place for it in the market. Her job is to find it.

"Chefs want three things: consistency, quality, timely delivery," she says. She's been known to load a bus with chefs and drive them from farm to farm, so they can see what's involved in bringing a product to their table.

One major hurdle has been marketing the entire animal. "Everybody wants high-end cuts of bison, but that's only 17 per cent of the animal. What's a producer to do with the other 83 per cent?" She wonders if consumers understand how fragile agriculture is. "I hope people will ask questions," she says. "I hope sometime they'll be willing to pay more to support locally grown product."

The Kuhlman family: Do Not Pave This Farm

Dietrich Kuhlmann and his family have been growing vegetables along 167th Avenue just north of Edmonton for 43 years. With about 300 acres of the richest topsoil in the province, it's a great spot for a garden.

In summer, Anne and Dietrich and their kids take 25 to 30 varieties of fresh vegetables to market, just hours out of the field. His two daughters, Angie and Anita, both married local farmers, and they're all partners in the family business.

However, the amount of fertile land between Kuhlmann's and the encroaching subdivisions is shrinking fast. He talks about the mounds and mounds of good soil already scraped up beside 167th Avenue.

Dietrich finds the encroaching development distressing, but he does see both sides of this debate. Some of his own neighbours want to subdivide their land for housing. "People need to be able to realize the true value for their property, and we can't stand in the way of that," he says. "Certain development rights should be given to the land owner. Ravines can't be farmed, they have a good view. Why not develop them for country residential?"

It's the deep-pocket developers who worry him. They want to flatten it all and pave it over. He just hopes they remember that once it's paved, it's gone forever.

He's not giving up. There's still a chance to save some big pieces of open land. "They're already zoned for agriculture. Our city councillors can restrict development. It's in their hands."

RIP

The reality of guidebooks is that even the best of businesses can fold or change. In order to keep our information as timely as possible, we include, a list of those good spots from Volume One that are either no longer in business, or are no longer open to the public.

This book is cross-indexed with the first *Food Lover's Trail Guide to Alberta*. Numbers following "V1" refer to page numbers in Volume 1. Numbers following "V2" refer to pages in this book.

LISTINGS BY CATEGORY

Restaurants, Cafés, Bistros, Diners & Neighbourhood Joints

ALPHABETICAL LISTING

B

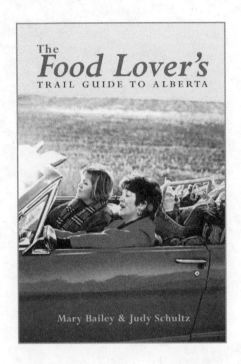

The
Food Lover's
TRAIL GUIDE TO ALBERTA

Mary Bailey & Judy Schultz

Celebrate Alberta! *The Food Lover's Trail Guide to Alberta*
will make even the armchair traveller hungry for the road.
This is the motherlode of appetizing information
—a must for every glove box, briefcase and bookshelf.

Where to find:
🐚 the cafés, bistros, diners and neighbourhood joints
🐚 the best home-grown ingredients
🐚 the most exotic and hard-to-find pantry items
🐚 the culinary shops and cooking schools
🐚 great restaurants for big nights, splurges and celebrations
🐚 harvest festivals, farmers markets, U-picks

**Plus the tastemakers, the food artisans, the chefs,
the sausage king and the giant pyrohy!**

"Tuck this book in your car and travel around Alberta with two women who clearly love good food and the passionate people who prepare it. *The Food Lover's Trail Guide* is a motherlode of local and regional discoveries. . . . What a treat!"

—Barbara Dacks, *Legacy*

"Alberta could hardly do better than to have Mary Bailey and Judy Schultz as topographers of its culinary landscape. [They] bring such an exhaustive knowledge of food to *The Food Lover's Trail Guide to Alberta*, you'd be lucky to exploit even half its contents in a year. . . . With *The Food Lover's Trail Guide* as a road map, foodies will find unbeaten paths to venture down, equipped with the inside scoop. And Bailey and Schultz's informed, all-embracing approach to their topic will ensure that readers come away from their book with more than just a well-whetted appetite."

—Scott Lingley, *Alberta Views*

"It will be tucked into my glove compartment from here on out—and now that warm weather has arrived, it will be a great way to add some interest to those summer road trips."

—Julie Pithers, *FFWD*

"A paperback bible for those searching out the best food the province has to offer."

—Lorena D. Johnson, *Calgary Sun*

"Sure to whet the insatiable Albertan appetite for travel—and for the wonderful food this province has to offer."

—Joanne Sasvari, *Calgary Herald*

"If you plan on taking to the highways this summer, *The Food Lover's Trail Guide to Alberta* in your glove box will be as indispensable as a road map."

—Marc Horton, *Edmonton Journal*

MARY BAILEY publishes *City Palate, the Flavour of Edmonton's Food Scene*. Her background is in hospitality and wine. She's a former board member of Cuisine Canada and is the founder of the Slow Food Convivium for Edmonton and northern Alberta.

JUDY SCHULTZ a nationally recognized food and travel writer, is the author of eight books and the winner of numerous awards. Her work appears in the *Edmonton Journal*. Judy lives near Edmonton with her husband and two amazing dogs, and spends her time cooking, gardening and dithering over her next writing project.

The authors are currently planning a series of international culinary tours that will bring offshore guests to sample Alberta's culinary riches.

ACKNOWLEDGEMENTS

We thank the growers, ranchers, producers, chefs and other food people who were so generous with their time and information, answering our questions at all hours, during the middle of their busy days to after midnight. We're also grateful to the *Edmonton Journal*, Anglo Canadian Motors for the use of the Jaguar that graces this cover, and the individuals and agencies who kindly gave us permission to use their file photos.